*Cooking*
*into*
EUROPE

# COOKING INTO EUROPE

*Contributors*

MARY NORWAK
JANE GRIGSON
MARI ESCRITT
MAGGIE BLACK

*Introduction by Clement Freud*

WARD LOCK LIMITED · LONDON
*in association with*
BRITISH GAS

# Introduction

My relationship with this book is pleasantly confused. When *Cooking into Europe* was first conceived, the plan was that I should review it. I had in my mind an opening paragraph in which I set myself up as a culinary Professor Higgins urging the reader to 'take a potato and work at it for 25 minutes', at which point I would announce the nationality of the cook. If it had been ignited, she was French; potato, wrapped in pasta and served with tomato, denotes the Italian approach. Braise the tuber in beer and you are a Luxemburger; the Dutch smoke it, Scandinavians salt it, Belgians name a festival in its honour and hurl it at passing floats. The Irish kneel down and bless their taties while the English boil them in unseasoned water. Germans ask for a second helping.

I was then asked to lunch with the editors and requested to contribute the chapter on Liechtenstein's cuisine, a task eminently within my capabilities, having regard to the fact that space in this volume was to be allocated according to the size of the country in question. Even this was not to be: Liechtenstein decided once again to go it alone and there was not much left for me but to opt for the introduction.

The American way of life, and I have considerable experience thereof, consists of ever more determined steps to give consumers across 50 states predictable, unprovocative, unobjectionably Republican food. The credo is that a Rhode Island cheeseburger must be indistinguishable from its cousins available in Hawaii or Alaska. Go where you will and qualitatively, quantitatively, even economically there is a high degree of acceptability, a limited amount of rapture. Ingredients are: a bun which will be white and soft; meat, unadulterated and bland; ketchup, sharp; pickle, fashioned of cucumber and sugar; cheese, processed; mustard standing by, along with a paper napkin and a glass of iced water.

Apart from the comparative cheeseburgerlessness of the Continent, one of the charms of Europe, gastronomically, lies in the very short distance you need travel to discover completely different approaches to the arts of the kitchen. In Texas you can buy a three-foot frankfurter at dawn and then drive fast along the national highway for twelve hours, by which time you are not only still in Texas but the three-foot frankfurter sign blinks at you resolutely in the gathering dusk.

In Europe the distance between 'cuisines' need be no farther than a gallop across a vineyard, on one side of which the speciality is luxuriantly fat snails, served with herb butter; on the other, non-snail side they break up Burgundy barrels and barbeque meat over the glowing vineous embers.

Before the latest three signatories to the treaty of Rome, there was, from the highest gastronomic standpoint, a certain lack of breadth, a culinary imbalance about the cuisines of original members. 'The Six' were Teuto-Gallic, desperately needing the Anglo-Irish-Scandinavian influence of the 1973 débutantes to become truly European. This they now have become . . . and while there is a lukewarm case for inviting Turkey or Bulgaria to contribute their 'Yoghourt über Alles' philosophy, even bring in Greece for its vineleaves and Spain for its paella, all but an ultra pedantic would have to admit that what we now have is as

Eel soup
*Lasagne al forno Bolognese*
Carp with raisin sauce
*Roti de veau à la creme*
Pigeon Pie
Liptauer cheese
Danish pastries
Irish coffee

comprehensive a selection of foods as a fastidious polyglot gourmet could desire.

Clearly there are two ways of using a compendium like this. One is to go haywire and design menus such as diplomatic chefs would be forced to prepare at meetings where no one nation must appear to be favoured over another; something like the adjacent menu.

The other is to vary one's national diet: to have Danish, Belgian or Italian week, or day, or meal, as do some restaurants with spectacular success. There is a lot to be said for both approaches, though in the fullness of time there is little doubt that each country will contribute quality items for the delectation of Common Market gourmets, and remove from its larders such monstrosities as stuffed larks, barbecued faggots and Danish Blue Cheese soufflé, and when the attendants on French railway station buffets start serving a steak, kidney and oyster pudding or stargazey pie, international gastronomy will have truly arrived. With the barriers down, and the borders open, the head waiter's 'haven't got any of that stuff' will finally manifest incompetence, not unavailability.

There is one great danger. This book, read with the care and love with which every serious work on cookery should be read, will show you how to prepare foods of different countries. But, however carefully you read (say) the chapter on the Netherlands, do not think that this qualifies you to advertise your services as a fully trained Dutch cook.

There is an idea, much believed in on the Continent, that when a person travels to another country his great desire is to eat the food of his own country. Just as every Australian is said to want to marry a deaf and dumb nymphomaniac who keeps a pub, so most English are, quite erroneously, believed to think that heaven is a fish and chip shop in the sun. This book should go a long way towards dispelling this myth. It might even cause Italians to appreciate that heaven need not be all that far from the fish and chip shop in the sun, provided they import a sufficiency of English malt vinegar and an adequate supply of the more popular British Sunday papers. I was once given a fillet of skate wrapped in *Le Figaro*; and for all its undoubted qualities as a great newspaper, it seemed to me there was something very seriously missing.

One thing that this book has taken pains to point out: cooking is simple; unless you cook for therapeutic reasons and your psychiatrist feels that three hours a day spinning sugar is the cure for your ailments, there must be a connection between time spent among the pots and pipkins, and the quality of the end product. Nothing in this book is going to take an outrageous amount of time; in fact everything, as Sherlock Holmes might have said, is 'alimentary, my dear Watson'. This last phrase could be difficult to translate.

When this book was being planned, Norway was odds on to join the EEC. Soon after the Norwegian chapter was completed, the people of that country decided to retain their independence, which left the editors in a quandary. This book could have been called *The Common Market and Norwegian Cookbook*; we could have torn out the relevant pages or requested you not to look at them. However, the editors, whose opinion is final, decided to leave them in, feeling that the recipes will provide housewives with much pleasure.

Clement Freud

# Contents

# *Belgium*

Belgian food is thought of as being based on braised cabbage, eels and mussels, diced pork, sliced thick sausage, the winter-warming stews often labelled *à la flamande*, and delicious pastries, pancakes and waffles. We think of apples, cider, and above all, beer. But Belgium's food is, more than all this, the food of festivals. There is probably no country in Europe with more carnivals, processions, pilgrimages, and ceremonial customs; all are reflected in the gaiety and cosmopolitan conventions of her diet; not surprisingly, since here is the Common Market's organisational centre too, where the experts from 'The Ten' all work, play – and eat.

One feature is the great Gilles carnival when thousands of oranges are scattered among the people, in memory of the conquest of Peru; then there is Krakelingenwerp, the 'Throwing of Biscuits', which recalls the miracle of the Loaves and Fishes. There is the Blessing of the Fields at Hakendover on Easter Monday to increase the harvest, and the Hops Festival symbolising its end. Best of all is the Feast of Wine and Grapes which comes just at the start of September, and the October Feeston, a huge feast of spit-roasted chickens, sausages and beer.

Although Belgium is a small country with close neighbours in France and Holland, the native food is highly original, and owes little to foreign influence. Excellent dishes are made from home-grown red cabbage, asparagus, chicory and sprouts, and these vegetables are known all over Europe for their Belgian origins.

Meat and fish dishes tend to be strongly flavoured and hearty. There are many varieties of sausage and black pudding, sometimes served cooked with hot red cabbage. Meat is often cooked in highly seasoned beer, and poultry and game may be paired with onions and rich sauces. There is always plenty of cream, butter and cheese for sauces, so that the food is rich and filling.

The baking of delicious sweet morsels plays a large part in the cooking of Belgium. Large open tarts with sweet creamy fillings are popular; spicy fruit breads, crisp spice biscuits, waffles and pancakes. Here and there too, are traces of colonial Congolese cooking, using bananas, mangoes, millet and peanuts, but these are naturally more popular in the towns.

# Belgium

## BELGIAN FISH SOUP
## WATERZOOI DE POISSON

*8 helpings*

*Ingredients*

4 pounds fish (eel, perch,
tench, carp, pike, etc.)
½ pound white or green celery
Salt and pepper
Bouquet garni (parsley,
thyme, bay leaves, 2-3 sage
leaves)
Fish stock or water
3½ ounces butter
Rusk crumbs, powdered

METHOD Clean the fish, and cut it into pieces 2-3 inches long. Wash the celery, and scrape and trim it if necessary. Chop it very finely or mince it. Butter a saucepan or stew pan, and put in the celery and the fish sections. Season with salt and pepper and the bouquet garni. Cover with the fish stock or water, and add the butter cut in small pieces. Cover the pan, and boil the soup briskly so that the liquor is reduced and thickened when the fish is cooked. Before serving, remove the bouquet garni and add the rusk crumbs to thicken the soup.

## MUSSELS
## MOULES

*Choose heavy, tightly closed mussels. To open them, put them in a pan without water, over low heat. As they warm, the shells will open. Beard, wash and scrape them before cooking.*

METHOD To cook them, remove them from their shells, place them in a pan and strain their liquor over them. Cook for 5 minutes. Drain well, if required.
  Use the mussels in one of the ways described below.

## MUSSELS 'AU GRATIN'
## MOULES AU GRATIN

*4-6 helpings*

*Ingredients*

4 pints mussels
1 onion, peeled and chopped
1 bay leaf
Thyme
Parsley
A few cooked mushrooms
Béchamel sauce
Butter
Browned breadcrumbs
Grated cheese

METHOD Open the mussels. Put them in a casserole or pan with their liquor and the onion, bay leaf, thyme and parsley. Cook them for about 5 minutes. Drain them, reserving the liquor. Put them in a fireproof dish. Slice the mushrooms thinly, and cover the mussels with them.
  Make a thick Béchamel sauce (see French section) using half milk and half mussel liquor. Spread the sauce over the mussels. Dot with butter, and sprinkle with the browned crumbs, then with a little grated cheese. Brown and heat the dish briefly under the grill.

## OMELET WITH MUSSELS
## OMELETTE AUX MOULES

METHOD Open as many mussels as wanted, as described under Mussels. Slice and mix with finely chopped parsley and chives to suit your taste. Add them to beaten, seasoned eggs and make an omelet in the usual way.

*Chicory and ham has a
crisp cheese topping.*

## CHICORY WITH HAM
## CHICORÉES AU JAMBON GRATINÉES

**4 helpings**

### Ingredients

METHOD Remove any discoloured leaves from the heads of the chicory. Trim the stumps if necessary. Wash the heads. Put them in a saucepan, with the juice of the lemon, a pinch of salt and the water. Cover the saucepan, and boil the chicory quickly for 15 minutes.

Let the heads cool, drain them and press the water out. Roll each head in a slice of ham. Arrange the rolls neatly in a shallow serving dish, and cover the whole dish with the sauce. Sprinkle well with the grated cheese, and set the dish in a moderately heated oven for 10 minutes.

*2 pounds chicory*
*1 lemon*
*Pinch of salt*
*4 fluid ounces water*
*4-8 slices cold, cooked (boiled) ham*
*Thick white sauce for coating*
*1 ounce Gruyère cheese, grated*

**GM 4 350°F 180°C**

# Belgium

## VEAL KIDNEY LIÈGEOISE
## ROGNON DE VEAU À LA LIÈGEOISE

*1 helping*

*Ingredients*

*1 veal kidney with fat*
*Salt and pepper*
*1 ounce butter*
*A few juniper berries,*
*crushed*
*1 tablespoon veal gravy or*
*strong chicken stock or*
*bouillon*
*1 small wineglass (3 fluid*
*ounces) gin, warmed and*
*flamed*

**GM 3 325°F**
**170°C**

METHOD Trim the kidney and cut off most of the fat; leave just a thin layer of fat round it. Snip out the core.

Light the oven. Put the butter in an earthenware dish or small casserole. Melt the butter by placing the dish or casserole in the oven. Put the kidney, well seasoned with salt and pepper, into the hot dish, replace the dish in the oven, and let the kidney simmer slowly until tender and cooked through; turn it often during cooking (the time will depend on the size of the kidney).

Just before serving, add the crushed juniper berries, gravy or stock and the flamed gin to the dish, and mix them in.

## FLEMISH BEEF AND ONION STEW
## CARBONNADES À LA FLAMANDE

METHOD Cut the beef into 1½-ounce pieces. Season with salt and pepper. Brown the pieces quickly in the butter or lard, turning them to brown them on all sides. Remove the meat from the pan, and take it off the heat.

Peel and mince or finely chop the onions. Brown them in the fat in the pan. Remove them. Place the pieces of beef and the onions in alternate layers in a saucepan. Pour in most of the stock or bouillon and the beer.

Add the flour to the fat in the pan. Fry it until brown, and moisten it with the reserved stock or bouillon. Simmer to thicken. Stir the thickened stock into the liquid in the saucepan. Season with the sugar. Cover the saucepan, and cook gently for 2½ hours.

### Ingredients

*1½ pounds lean stewing steak*
*Salt and pepper*
*4 ounces butter or lard*
*1 pound onions*
*½ pint stock or beef bouillon*
*½ pint beer*
*2 ounces flour*
*1 tablespoon brown sugar*

## CHICKEN, GHENT STYLE
## WATERZOOI DE POULET GANTOISE

*4 helpings*

METHOD Prepare the chicken for poaching. Make the julienne by trimming, scraping and washing the carrot, leeks and celery, and cutting all the vegetables into matchsticks. Put the chicken and julienne into a saucepan, cover with 4 pints boiling water, and poach for 45 minutes.

Take out the chicken and vegetables. Keep the cooking liquid.

Make a *roux* by melting the butter, adding the flour and cooking them together for a few moments without browning. Add enough cooking liquor, gradually, to make a pouring sauce. Add the cream, and then the beaten egg yolks; remove the sauce from the heat at once and stir the cream and eggs in, to thicken it. If necessary, return to the heat for a moment or two but on no account let the sauce boil. When it is thickened, keep it warm by standing the container in a pan of hot water.

Cut the chicken into neat pieces, removing the bones and skin. Put the chicken pieces, vegetables and sauce into a deep dish for serving. Serve with boiled potatoes.

### Ingredients

*1 tender 3-pound chicken*
**Julienne** *of vegetables (see*
  *below)*
*1 ounce of butter*
*1½ ounces flour*
*¼ pint single cream*
*2 egg yolks*
**For the Julienne**
*1 carrot*
*2 ounces mushrooms*
*2 leeks*
*2 stalks white celery*

# Belgium

## APPLE TURNOVER
## CHAUSSON AUX POMMES

**Ingredients**

*Pastry*
*8 ounces flour*
*4 ounces butter*
*½ ounce castor sugar*
*Pinch of salt*
*7½ fluid ounces water*
*2 egg yolks*
*Filling*
*2 pounds sharp dessert apples*
*1 whole egg, beaten*
*Sugar to glaze*

GM 7 425°F   GM 8 450°F
220°C        230°C

METHOD Mix the flour with the butter, rubbing in the latter until the mixture is like fine breadcrumbs. Work in the sugar, salt, water and egg yolks gradually kneading with the heel of the hand. Roll the pastry together, and knead again. Roll into a ball, and leave in a cool dry place for 2 hours. Peel, core and stew the apples with the least possible amount of water. Leave them to cool.

Roll the pastry into a ½-inch thick circle. Put the stewed apples in the centre, dampen the edges of the pastry and fold it in half. Seal the edges together, and make a little border with your fingers. Cover the surface by brushing on a film of beaten egg. Bake in a hot oven until the pastry is firm and cooked through. When it is nearly done, sprinkle with the sugar, and raise the heat to glaze it. Leave to cool before serving.

## WHITE CHEESECAKE
## TARTE AU FROMAGE BLANC

**Ingredients**

*6 ounces flaky pastry*
*1 pound unsalted white curd cheese*
*2 ounces castor sugar*
*Pinch of salt*
*½ ounce flour*
*2 egg yolks*
*2 tablespoons melted butter*
*2 whipped egg whites*
*Crushed loaf or granulated sugar to glaze*

GM 7 425°F   GM 8 450°F
220°C        230°C

METHOD Line a shallow 8-inch flan ring or pie plate with the pastry. Crumble the cheese into a basin and work in the sugar, salt, flour, egg yolks and butter. Stir in 1 tablespoon of whipped egg white, then fold in the rest. Fill the tart with this mixture. Bake in a hot oven until firm in the centre. Shortly before the end of the cooking time, sprinkle with the extra sugar and raise the heat to glaze the tart.

# Belgium

## LIÉGE RICE CAKE
## TARTE AU RIZ LIÉGEOISE

METHOD Grease an 8-inch flan ring or pie plate and line it with the pastry. Bring the milk to the boil, toss in the rice, and stir once. Add 1 pinch of salt. Bring back to the boil, stirring all the time with a wooden spoon. When the milk has risen, add the second pinch of salt, the cinnamon and sugar. Cook for 30 minutes, just simmering, until the rice is very tender. Dilute with the little cold milk, then whisk in the cornflour and egg yolks. Whisk well. Allow the mixture to thicken, but do not let it boil again. When it thickens, remove the pan from the heat and fold in the stiffly beaten whites. Pour this mixture evenly on to the pastry. Brush with the beaten egg and castor sugar. Bake in a hot oven for about 30 minutes. The surface of the tart should be golden-brown. Leave to cool, then sprinkle with the fine castor sugar.

### Ingredients

6 ounces flaky pastry
1½ pints milk
5 ounces washed, drained rice
2 pinches salt
Large pinch of ground cinnamon
6 ounces castor sugar
A little cold milk
1 tablespoon cornflour
3 egg yolks
3 stiffly whipped egg whites
Beaten egg and castor sugar
Fine castor sugar

GM 7 425°F
220°C

## SUGAR TART
## TARTE AU SUCRE

METHOD Rub the butter or margarine into the flour. Add the egg, sugar, salt and cinnamon and work in well. Blend the yeast with enough warm milk and add to make a fairly solid dough. Cover and leave to rise in a warm place, to twice its volume. Knead again, then roll out into a ½-inch thick circle.

Grease a large pie plate thoroughly, and cover it with the dough. Roll over the top to remove any surplus.

Beat the egg with 3 tablespoons sugar and cinnamon. Spread this mixture on the dough, and sprinkle with the remaining castor sugar. Make a few incisions in the surface of the tart to give it air. Leave to rise again. Bake the tart in a very hot oven for 20-25 minutes. Cool on a wire rack.

### Ingredients

**Dough**
8 ounces flour
4 ounces butter or margarine
1 egg
½ ounce of fresh yeast
Warm milk
1 tablespoon castor sugar
Pinch of salt
Pinch of cinnamon

**For the topping**
1 egg
4 tablespoons castor or soft brown sugar
½ teaspoon ground cinnamon

GM 8 450°F
230°C

## BRUSSELS CAKES
## CAKES DE BRUXELLES

METHOD Put the eggs, egg yolks and sugar in the top of a double boiler, over hot water. Place the boiler over heat, and stir until the mixture is smooth and thick, like mayonnaise. Remove from the heat, and mix in thoroughly the flour and fruit. Prepare 24-30 small, buttered, greaseproof paper cases. Fill them with the mixture. Bake in a moderate oven until firm. This takes about 30 minutes.

One large cake may be made in a 10-inch tin. The preparation is the same, but it will take 1 hour to bake.

### Ingredients

6 eggs
4 egg yolks
14 ounces castor sugar
14 ounces flour, sifted
8 ounces finely chopped preserved fruit (raisins, candied orange and lemon peel, angelica etc.)

GM 4 350°F
180°C

# Denmark

Although three-quarters of Denmark's population live in towns today, few are more than a generation or two away from farming. Most people know of someone who is still farming, or associated with the production of dairy produce, bacon or canned foods.

Country folk know all about good food of the highest quality, so that traditional Danish dishes feature dairy and pork products prepared in simple but original ways.

The Danes not only love food, but they love parties. Difficult travelling in past years encouraged the growth of hospitality for weary guests, when a welcoming meal was an occasion. Today, Denmark is famous for its Cold Table, presented with a cook's skill and an artist's eye, and equally appropriate for the relaxed family meal, or the more formal party. The same skill is employed in the making of Open Sandwiches, when everyday ingredients are used to make tempting and nourishing morsels which provide lunch for millions of Danes, and for the intricate and delicious Danish Pastries.

Perhaps the beautiful presentation of food was encouraged by the many French cooks who travelled to Scandinavia in centuries gone by. Not only must individual dishes be beautiful to look at, but the table must be exquisitely set with elegant china, candles and flowers. Joints of meat are skilfully carved ahead of a meal, arranged on the serving platter with colourful vegetables. The cheeseboard comes with slices ready to serve, and appropriate accompaniments of crisp salad vegetables, fruit and nuts. Eating in Denmark is a stimulating experience.

Happily it can be shared by other countries, for there is also a strong tradition of food export, and people outside Denmark have come to expect the highest quality from Danish produce. Butter, bacon and eggs are now joined by salami, ham, smoked pork loin and chickens, by shrimps, cod's roe and pickled herrings, and by Havarti, Samsoe, Mycella, Danish Blue and a host of other cheeses. To complete our taste of Danish hospitality, there is lager and the celebrated *Akvavit* ('snaps').

# Denmark

## OPEN SANDWICHES
## SMØRREBRØD

*In Denmark it takes three years to learn to make a sandwich, since young girls take that time to serve an apprenticeship which will qualify them as approved sandwich makers. One restaurant in Copenhagen has a sandwich list which is four feet long, with nearly 200 varieties offered. Two or three sandwiches make a meal with a glass of lager or a cup of coffee. The sandwiches have to be tackled with a knife and fork, since they consist of a single slice of thin bread with a variety of toppings laid on thinly, thickly or toweringly, presenting a feast to the eye and to the palate.*

*Bread*

The bread should be fresh with a good crust, and close-textured to take the weight of the topping. Danish rye bread is the ideal base, about $\frac{1}{8}$ of an inch thick. Delicate flavours such as mild cheese, chicken and shrimps, are best on white bread. White bread should be about $\frac{1}{4}$ inch thick, and the slices should be 2 inches by 4 inches, or approximately half a slice from a large sandwich loaf.

*Butter*

The bread should be completely covered with a good spreading of Danish butter which goes on evenly and thickly to provide a moisture-proof seal to the bread and a firm anchorage for the topping.

*Toppings*

The topping of a sandwich should be of ample proportions to cover the bread completely. Generally, one major ingredient such as ham or cheese is used liberally, to be finished with appropriate garnishes. Meats and some cheeses can be folded or rolled to add height.

*Garnishes*

Appropriate garnishes should be chosen to add colour and complementary flavouring. The effect of the sandwich should be fresh and bright, but not over-ornamental or fussy. A lettuce leaf, parsley sprig or cress, onion rings, twists of cucumber, tomato or lemon can be used, or slightly more elaborate finishes such as:

RADISH ROSES Leave about $\frac{1}{2}$ inch of the green leaf. Cut the radish in sections from the base towards the stalk. Put in cold water to open.

TOMATO TWISTS Cut tomato slices through the centre of the core leaving a piece at the top holding the two halves together. Turn halves in opposite directions to make the twist.

SCRAMBLED EGG STRIPS Press scrambled egg lightly while it cools. When cold, cut neat strips as a garnish for ham, salami, canned meats and salad.

HORSERADISH SALAD Grate fresh horseradish into whipped cream. Flavour with lemon juice and a little sugar.

GHERKIN FAN Slice a gherkin several times for two-thirds of its length, leaving a joined portion at the stalk end. Press slices apart to form a fan.

# Denmark

*Danish open
sandwiches with
garnished toppings.*

# Denmark

*Serving*

Open sandwiches are served on a flat meat dish or tray from which they can be lifted with a palette knife or cake server. Usually a fish sandwich is served first (preferably with a glass of 'snaps' frosty-cold). Meat, poultry and cheese varieties follow.

*Sandwich Selection*

1 Pickled herring with onion rings, lettuce and tomato on rye bread.
2 Shrimps on a bed of lettuce, topped with a lemon slice on white bread.
3 Sliced hard-boiled egg with tomatoes sprinkled with chives on a bed of lettuce on rye bread.
4 Smoked salmon and scrambled eggs sprinkled with chives on white bread.
5 Samsoe cheese with a twist of orange on white bread.
6 Danish Blue Cheese with black grapes and walnuts on white bread.
7 Drumstick of fried chicken on a bed of lettuce with fried bacon roll, tomato, cucumber and watercress on white bread.
8 Roast beef in thin slices with onion rings and gherkins on rye bread.
9 Rounds of Danish salami and onion rings with parsley on rye bread.
10 Liver paste and butter-fried mushroom slices with bacon and lettuce on rye bread.
11 Ham with tomato, cucumber and a strip of scrambled egg with chives on white bread.
12 Cold roast pork with red cabbage. prunes, an orange slice and a piece of pork crackling and lettuce on rye bread.

## LIVER PASTE
## OVNBAGT LEVERPOSTEJ

*12 helpings*

*This liver paste is very smooth and creamy, with a touch of anchovy, and is firmer than most pâtés. It is used in slices for the Cold Table, or for open sandwiches, and is very good eaten with pickled cucumbers.*

### Ingredients

12 ounces pig's liver
8 ounces pork fat
5 anchovy fillets
1 small onion
2 ounces dry breadcrumbs
1 ounce butter
1 ounce plain flour
½ pint milk
1 egg
1 teaspoon salt
1 teaspoon pepper
1 teaspoon mixed spice
1 teaspoon ground cloves
½ teaspoon sugar
12 ounces ⅛-inch strips of pork fat

GM 350°F
180°C

METHOD Mince liver, pork fat, anchovy fillets and onion on fine blade three times. Soak breadcrumbs in a little of the milk. Melt butter, work in flour, add milk, and cook together to make a thick white sauce. Cool and stir in the egg and seasonings. Mix sauce thoroughly into the liver mixture until smoothly blended, together with the breadcrumbs.

Line 1½-pound loaf tin or terrine with strips of pork fat so that they overlap slightly and cover the bottom and sides of the container. Put liver mixture into container and cover with strips of pork fat. Cover with a double thickness of cooking foil. Put container into a baking tin half-full of water. Bake in moderate oven for 1½ hours. Remove foil, and chill thoroughly before serving.

# Denmark

## YELLOW PEA SOUP
## GULE AERTER

*6 helpings*

*The Danish national soup, almost a meal in itself. The meat is often served separately with pickled beetroot, mustard, rye bread and butter, akvavit and lager.*

METHOD Soak the peas overnight. Next day boil them in three pints of unsalted water until tender. Simmer the pork separately with a bouquet of herbs and the other vegetables. When the pork is tender, remove from the pot and keep hot. Then sieve the peas and add to the pork broth, from which all fat has been removed. Serve the pork with the soup. Small potatoes may be added to the soup during the last 20 minutes of cooking time if a more substantial dish is desired.

### Ingredients

*1 pound dried yellow peas*
*2 pounds salt pork*
*3 pints water*
*3-4 carrots*
*4 onions*
*1-2 leeks*
*Bouquet garni*

# Denmark

### PLAICE WITH MUSHROOMS
### RØDSPAETTE MED CHAMPIGNONER

*8 helpings*

*Plaice is a popular fish, although rather expensive.*

**Ingredients**
*8 plaice fillets*
*Egg and breadcrumbs to coat*
*4 ounces butter*
*8 ounces mushrooms*
*½ pint single cream*
*Lemon juice*
*Tomato purée*
**GM 5 375°F**
**190°C**

METHOD Lightly season plaice fillets, dip them in egg and bread-crumbs, and then put them in a buttered oven-proof dish. Dot with knobs of butter (about 2 ounces) and bake in a fairly hot oven until fish is nicely golden for about 20 minutes. Remove from oven. Meanwhile, lightly cook mushrooms in butter, then stir in the cream mixed with a little lemon juice and tomato purée. Pour this sauce over the fish and return to the oven for a few minutes. Serve with creamed potatoes.

*Plaice with mushrooms.*

### BACON AND EGG CAKE
### FLAESKEAEGGEKAGE

*3-4 helpings*

*Bacon and egg cake is a Danish favourite for a first course, a light lunch or supper dish. It is cooked slowly on top of the cooker until it has set to a custard-like consistency, and topped with crisp bacon and a snipping of chopped chives. It is always served straight from the frying pan.*

**Ingredients**
*8 ounces back bacon rashers*
*1 tablespoon plain flour*
*6 tablespoons milk*
*4 eggs*
*Salt and pepper*
*½ ounce butter*
*Parsley or chives*

METHOD Remove the rinds from the bacon rashers. Put the rashers under a medium grill and cook until golden brown and crisp (3-4 minutes). Blend together the flour and milk until smooth, then beat in the eggs and season with salt and pepper. Put butter into a frying pan and heat until just turning brown. Pour in the egg mixture, and cook over a fairly high heat until just set, lifting the edges occasionally (5-6 minutes). Put cooked bacon rashers on top and garnish with chopped parsley or chives.

*Bacon and egg-cake
with tomatoes.*

## ROAST PORK WITH APPLES AND PRUNES
## STEGT SVINEKAM MED AEBLER OG SVESKER

*12 helpings*

*Rich meats such as pork and goose are traditionally served
with a stuffing or garnish of apples and prunes which provide
a delicious contrast to the flavour of the meat and help to
cut the richness.*

METHOD Put prunes into a saucepan, cover with cold water, and
bring to the boil. Remove from heat and leave the prunes to
soak for 30 minutes. Drain and dry. Peel and core apple, cut into
1-inch cubes, and sprinkle with lemon juice. With a long skewer,
make a tunnel in the pork running the length of the loin, and
season lightly with salt and pepper. Using the fingers, insert

### Ingredients
*5 pounds boned loin of pork
12 medium-sized stoned prunes
1 large cooking apple
1 teaspoon lemon juice
Salt and pepper*

23

prunes and apple pieces alternately, and push them through the meat, using the long handle of a wooden spoon. Make sure the loin is tied securely at 1-inch intervals. Roast in moderate oven for 2 hours. Pork should be well-done. Serve with sugar-browned potatoes (see opposite page).

**GM 4 350°F**
**180°C**

*Roast pork with apples and prunes.*

**12 helpings**

## ROAST GOOSE WITH APPLES AND PRUNES
## GAASESTEG MED AEBLER OG SVESKER

*The traditional bird eaten on Christmas Eve. It is best to use a young goose for this dish, which should be garnished with poached apple halves stuffed with prunes soaked in port. Appropriate vegetables are red cabbage and sugar-browned potatoes.*

**Ingredients**
*1 8-pound goose*
*½ lemon*
*Salt and pepper*
*1 pound crisp apples*
*8 ounces prunes*
*1 ounce butter*
*1 ounce plain flour*
*4 ounces redcurrant jelly*

**GM 8 450°F  GM 4 350°F**
**230°C      180°C**

METHOD Wipe and dry goose and rub with lemon inside and out. Sprinkle inside and out with salt and pepper. Core and chop apples and mix with prunes which have been soaked, stoned and chopped. Stuff goose and secure with skewer or sew the opening. Prick goose all over lightly with a fork and put on rack in roasting tin. Use an oven already preheated to a very high temperature. Put in goose, and turn down heat to a moderate level. Roast for 25 minutes per pound, pouring off fat as it accumulates in the pan, and basting goose occasionally. Put goose on a hot serving dish. Drain fat from pan, leaving only meat juices. Add enough water to make up a pint, and heat gently. Cream butter and flour together, and stir into liquid. Stir in redcurrant jelly and heat through. Serve sauce separately.

# Denmark

## SUGAR-BROWNED POTATOES
## BRUNEDE KARTOFLER

*4 helpings*

*Serve these potatoes with meat, poultry or ham.*

METHOD Cook potatoes in boiling water until tender. Drain and peel. Dissolve sugar in a strong saucepan over a gentle heat. Simmer till just beginning to turn golden. Add butter and allow to melt. Rinse potatoes in cold water. Then shake them gently in the sugar mixture until nicely glazed. Turn into a warm serving dish.

*Ingredients*
*20 small potatoes*
*2 tablespoons sugar*
*2 ounces butter*


## VEILED COUNTRY LASS
## BONDEPIGE MED SLØR

*6 helpings*

*This is a kind of apple dessert, best made with pumpernickel or very dark rye bread.*

METHOD Mix breadcrumbs, butter and sugar in a heavy frying pan and toss gently over medium heat until the breadcrumbs are very crisp. Leave to cool. Put alternate layers of crumbs and apple sauce in a serving dish, ending with breadcrumbs. Cover with whipped cream and decorate with redcurrant jelly. Chill before serving. Sometimes about 1 tablespoon grated plain chocolate is added to the breadcrumbs.

*Ingredients*
*1 pound fine rye breadcrumbs*
*1½ ounces butter*
*1 ounce sugar*
*1 pound thick apple sauce*
*½ pint double cream*
*1 tablespoon redcurrant jelly*


## LEMON SOUFFLÉ
## CITRONFROMAGE

*4 helpings*

METHOD Put the gelatine to dissolve in a little water. Beat egg yolks with lemon peel and sugar until white. Add lemon juice, the dissolved gelatine and finally the stiffly whipped egg whites and half the whipped cream. Stir carefully until the soufflé begins to stiffen. Pour into a prepared soufflé dish, and when set decorate with the rest of the whipped cream, piping it in a decorative pattern.

*Ingredients*
*2½ heaped teaspoons*
  *powdered gelatine*
*4 eggs*
*Grated peel of 1½ lemons*
*4 ounces sugar*
*Juice of 2 lemons*
*½ pint double cream*


## VANILLA WREATHS
## VANILLA KRANSE

*These are probably the most popular Danish biscuits.*

METHOD Work all ingredients together and let the dough stand for 20 minutes, in a cool place. Put into a pastry bag or tube and press into long thin rolls. Cut rolls in equal-size pieces and form into small rings on a well-greased baking tin. Bake in a fairly hot oven for 10 minutes until light brown.

*Ingredients*
*18 ounces plain flour*
*½ teaspoon baking powder*
*13 ounces butter*
*9 ounces sugar*
*4 ounces blanched, minced*
  *almonds*
*1 egg*
*3 drops vanilla essence*

**GM 6 400°F**
     **200°C**

# Denmark

## CURRANT BISCUITS
## KORENDEKAGER

**Ingredients**
7 ounces butter
7 ounces sugar
4 ounces currants
4 ounces plain flour
4 ounces desiccated coconut
2½ teaspoons baking powder

GM 6 400°F
200°C

METHOD Cream butter and sugar. Then add remaining ingredients and stir until smooth. Place dots of dough on well-greased baking tin with a teaspoon. Do not place too close as they spread while baking. Bake in fairly hot oven for 10 minutes until golden brown. Leave to cool on baking tin for a few minutes before removing.

## MEDALS
## MEDALJER

*These little cakes are a reward given as a special treat.*

**Ingredients**
3 ounces butter
1 egg yolk
4 ounces plain flour
¼ pint double cream
12 strawberries, hulled

METHOD Soften the butter, beat in the egg yolk and blend in the sifted flour. Knead well. Wrap dough and put in a cool place for 1-2 hours. Roll out thinly on a floured board. Cut out with a 1-inch plain round cutter, approximately 24 pieces. Place rounds on a baking sheet. Bake in fairly hot oven for 10 minutes until

*Christmas biscuits.*

pale golden brown. Cool medals on a wire rack.

Lightly whip the cream and use it to sandwich together the medals, reserving a little for the tops. Pipe a small dot of cream on each medal and decorate with the strawberries.

**GM 6 400°F**
**200°C**

## CHRISTMAS BISCUITS
## BRUNE KAGER

*These are particularly popular Christmas biscuits.*

METHOD Put butter, sugar and syrup into a saucepan and warm slowly. When this mixture reaches boiling point remove from the heat. Add chopped candied peel and almonds, and allow to cool until lukewarm. Then add the flour and spices, stirring with a wooden spoon, and knead to get a smooth dough.

Roll into cylinders 2 inches in diameter. Keep in a cool place until the next day. Cut the cylinders into thin slices. Place on a greased baking tray. Bake in fairly hot oven for 10-15 minutes until brown. Cool on a rack and put in an air-tight tin when cold.

*Ingredients*
*8 ounces butter*
*8 ounces sugar*
*4 ounces syrup*
*2 ounces almonds*
*2 ounces candied peel*
*1 pound plain flour*
*2 teaspoons ground cloves*
*3 teaspoons ground cinnamon*
*1 teaspoon ground ginger*

**GM 6 400°F**
**200°C**

## CUSTARD TARTS
## LINSER

METHOD Sieve the flour and work in the butter with the fingers. Add the sugar and egg yolks and mix all ingredients well. Handle the dough very carefully as it breaks easily. Roll out thinly, and use half to line deep tartlet tins. Make up custard and fill the cases. Cover with lids of dough and press edges together lightly. Bake in fairly hot oven for 10 minutes until golden brown. Cool in tins for 5 minutes, remove carefully, and cool before serving.

To make the custard, heat the milk. Beat together the sugar, flour, eggs and egg yolk. Add a little of the hot milk and mix well, then add remaining milk. Bring to the boil, stirring constantly. Cool, stirring often to prevent a skin forming, and flavour with vanilla essence before using.

*Ingredients*
*7 ounces plain flour*
*4 ounces butter*
*6 ounces castor sugar*
*2 egg yolks*
**For the custard**
*¾ pint milk*
*2 tablespoons sugar*
*2 tablespoons plain flour*
*2 eggs and 1 egg yolk*
*4 drops vanilla essence*

**GM 6 400°F**
**200°C**

## OTHELLO CAKE
## OTHELLO KAGE

METHOD Beat the butter and sugar together until creamy, add egg yolks one at a time and beat well. Fold in the flour and finally the stiffly beaten egg whites. Bake in well-greased 8-inch baking tin with a loose bottom in moderate oven for 45 minutes. When cold cut into three layers, and sandwich two together with custard cream. Spread on more custard cream and a layer of macaroons. Then more custard cream and the top layer of cake. Decorate the cake with chocolate water icing, and pipe with stiffly beaten cream.

To make the custard, beat the egg yolks, sugar and the cornflour. Bring the milk to the boil with the vanilla pod in it. Pour a little of the boiling milk into the egg mixture and return to the heat with the rest of the milk. Bring to boil, beating all the time. Remove from the heat and whisk until cold.

*Ingredients*
*5 ounces butter*
*7 ounces sugar*
*3 eggs, separated*
*7 ounces self-raising flour*
**Custard cream**
*3 egg yolks*
*2 tablespoons sugar*
*3 tablespoons cornflour*
*½ pint milk*
*½ vanilla pod*
*12 small almond macaroons*
**Chocolate water icing**
**Whipped cream**

**GM 4 350°F**
**180°C**

# Denmark

## DANISH PASTRIES
## WEINERBRØD

*These pastries take a little time and trouble, but are delicious with coffee. Fillings include jam, lemon curd, dried fruit, apple sauce, almond paste and vanilla custard.*

### Ingredients
6 ounces butter
8 ounces plain flour
Pinch of salt
½ ounce fresh yeast
5 tablespoons cold water
1 egg
½ ounce castor sugar
Fillings and decorations (see shaping instructions)

METHOD Take the butter out of the refrigerator before preparing the basic dough. Sieve together flour and salt. Cream yeast with cold water. Add the beaten egg and sugar to the yeast. Put this liquid into the flour, and work lightly to a soft smooth dough. Place dough in a greased plastic bag and leave in a cold place for 10 minutes.

Beat the butter with a wooden spoon to a spreading consistency and shape into a rectangle about ½-inch thick. Roll out the dough into a 10-inch square. Place butter in the centre. Fold sides over middle, overlapping them by $\frac{1}{2}$ inch. Seal ends. Roll into a strip approximately 18 inches by 6 inches and fold evenly into three. Cover and rest dough in a cold place for 10 minutes. Repeat rolling, folding and resting the dough twice more.

Shape the basic dough as required. Leave the pastries to prove in slight warmth until puffy. (Do not have the temperature too warm or the butter will run.) Bake in hot oven for 12-15 minutes. Allow to cool before decorating.

**GM 7 425°F
220°C**

## BUTTER HORNS

*Makes 8*

METHOD Take half the basic dough from the refrigerator and roll it out thinly into a circle about 12 inches in diameter. Trim edge, if necessary. Divide into eight sections. Brush the two long sides of each piece with beaten egg. Place a little of the almond paste in the middle of the short side. Roll up towards the point and curl into a crescent shape. Place on a greased baking sheet and brush over with beaten egg. Scatter the almonds on top. Prove about 10 minutes and bake.

*Ingredients*
*Filling*
*2 ounces almond paste*
*Decoration*
*½ ounce blanched chopped almonds*
*Little beaten egg*

## FRUIT SNAILS

*Makes 8*

METHOD Roll out the dough into a rectangle approximately 16 inches by 6 inches. Spread with spiced butter and scatter sultanas and finely chopped peel over. Roll up from the short end to make a fat roll. Cut it into $\frac{3}{4}$-inch slices and place on a baking sheet. Flatten slightly. Prove about 10 minutes and bake. Decorate with the water icing when cool.

*Ingredients*
*Filling*
*Spiced butter (cream 2 ounces butter, 2 ounces castor sugar, 2 level teaspoons cinnamon)*
*1 ounce sultanas*
*1 ounce mixed peel*
*Decoration*
*Water icing (2 ounces icing sugar, approx. 1 dessertspoon water)*

## WINDMILLS

*Makes 8*

METHOD Roll out the dough approximately 8 inches by 16 inches and cut into 4-inch squares. Put a little of the almond paste in the centre of each square. Brush the almond lightly with beaten egg. Cut from the corners of each square towards the middle. Fold corners of each triangular piece thus formed towards the centre and press the points into the almond paste firmly. Brush over with beaten egg. Prove about 10 minutes and bake. When cool, place raspberry jam in the centre of each 'windmill'.

*Ingredients*
*Filling*
*2 ounces almond paste*
*Decoration*
*Beaten egg*
*8 teaspoons raspberry jam*

## COCKS' COMBS

*Makes 8*

METHOD Roll out the dough approximately 8 inches by 16 inches and cut into 4-inch squares. Spread a teaspoon of the chosen filling across the centre of each square and fold over to make an oblong. Seal the edges together and make 8-10 incisions. Bend each Comb so that the 'teeth' fan out. Brush with egg and scatter with chopped almonds. Prove about 10 minutes and bake.

*Ingredients*
*Filling*
*3 ounces lemon curd or apple sauce*
*Decoration*
*Beaten egg*
*½ ounce chopped almonds*

# France

What are the flavours of France? The richness of olive oil, tomatoes, garlic, shallots and onions; the fragrance of parsley, basil, anise, tarragon and fennel; the piquant mustards, mild yet sharp wine vinegar, undeprived sea salt and freshly ground pepper? All these, but above all, the lovely combinations of wine and brandy married with butter, cream and eggs.

You need only look at a map of France to see how its culinary superiority was inevitable. Since Roman times, it has profited from the gardening skills of the Middle East and Italy. Through the Mediterranean have come spices and fruits from China and the Far East, and vegetables which we now accept as an essential part of our lives. None are native to France. And yet France has shown us how to use them to best advantage.

The map gives an idea of the variety of foods native to the country. The cream and butter of Normandy is matched by a total of over 300 local cheeses spanning the entire country. No meal is complete in France without cheese, which is always served before the dessert. Fish and seafood range from the lobsters of the cool Atlantic waters of the North to the squids of the Mediterranean. The great rivers flowing down from the mountains and the lakes provide an abundance of freshwater fish. The rich cornlands of the Beauce produce the fine flour that has helped make the French pastries, soufflés and pancakes so wonderfully light. The wines, brandies and liqueurs of France provide a true complement to any French meal.

During the Middle Ages, the *charcuteries,* or 'cooked pork shops' began to spring up in most of the small towns and larger villages. French housewives still depend on them for their ready-made delicacies including sausages, smoked meats, pâtés, pig's trotters and specialities made from minced tripe.

Carême, the hero of *haute cuisine,* summed up in his books written at the beginning of the 19th century the great strength of French cookery. Later, a host of restaurants were established by chefs to cater for the newly prosperous merchant and professional classes. A change in social habits resulted particularly when, under César Ritz and his chef Escoffier, restaurants became elegant enough to women to be seen in them. During this period pastry cooks in the smart districts of Paris invented cakes such as *Gâteau St Honoré* that have since become world famous. Social changes following the First World War led to a turning away from Paris and a revived interest in the cookery of the regions of France. Each area's simple, wholesome ingredients are given individual character by the addition of the subtle flavouring of local sauces and seasoning.

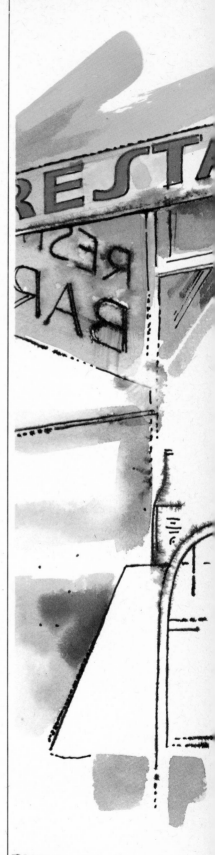

# France

## FRENCH SAUCES

*The range of French sauces is one of the glories of cookery. They were mainly developed in the 17th and 18th centuries (I have listed below some basic sauces, with most followed by suggested variations) when France came under the influence of Renaissance Italy. One doesn't always realise that this period produced not only fine paintings and sculpture and architecture, but also a new attitude towards cookery on account of the progress made in farming and gardening. These sauces often bear the names of the great men of France; this means that they were either invented or conspicuously improved by their chefs. Sauce* **Soubise,** *for instance, an onion sauce, was invented by Marin, chef to the Marquis de Soubise, whose exquisite palace you may still see in the Marais district of Paris. Béchamel, the Marquis Louis de Béchamel to name him correctly, was steward to Louis XIV.*

## BÉCHAMEL SAUCE

**Ingredients**
*Béchamel sauce*
*1 pint milk*
*Large slice onion*
*Piece of carrot*
*Bouquet garni*
*Grated nutmeg*
*2 good tablespoons butter*
*2 rounded tablespoons flour*
*Salt, pepper*

METHOD Simmer first five ingredients gently together for 10 minutes, just under boiling point. Melt butter in another pan, stir in flour and cook without colouring for two minutes. Strain in the hot flavoured milk to make a smooth sauce. Simmer, giving an occasional stir, until the sauce is reduced to the desired consistency. Season to taste.

SAUCE MORNAY Add grated cheese to basic Béchamel at the end of cooking. A mixture of Gruyère and Parmesan is best. A favourite sauce for dishes baked in the oven, *au gratin,* vegetables, certain meats, fish and so on. Sprinkle the top with more grated cheese, mixed with a few breadcrumbs, to give a nice brown finish. For extra piquancy, French mustard may also be stirred in at the end.

SAUCE SOUBISE Blanch 1 pound sliced onions for 5 minutes. Then drain and stew slowly with 2 ounces butter, and 1 glass of dry white wine, until reduced to a purée. Sieve into a fairly thick Béchamel, until the flavour appeals to you. For fish, lamb.

## VELOUTÉ SAUCE

*Velvet sauce or* velouté *was originally known as* **Béchamel grasse** *– i.e. fat Béchamel made with a meat stock. (Our Béchamel was called* **Béchamel maigre,** *lean Béchamel, because it was made with fish stock or plain milk for fast days.)*

METHOD Use meat stock, or fish stock with a glass of white wine, or half stock and half cream, instead of the milk given in the Béchamel recipe. Add mushroom trimmings with stock, if possible.

An extra velvety texture is produced by thickening the sauce with 2 egg yolks beaten up with 3 tablespoons of cream. A little hot sauce is poured on to this mixture, and the whole thing is returned to the pan and stirred for a few minutes over a gentle heat. It must not boil or the eggs will curdle.

Another way is to fork up a tablespoon of butter with a tablespoon of flour, and add the resulting paste (*beurre manié*) in little knobs to the sauce at the end. Stir over a moderate heat, without boiling, until the sauce is thicker and slightly glossy. A knob of butter added just before serving is a further improvement.

All the variations mentioned above for Béchamel, can be used with velouté. It is the ideal method to produce a mussel sauce for serving with white fish – use the liquid from opening the mussels to make the velouté, add the mussels finally.

## SAUCE MAYONNAISE

*No one is certain of the derivation of the word mayonnaise. The most usual explanation is that it was named in honour of the taking of Port-Mahon in Minorca by the Duc de Richelieu in 1756. The great French chef, Carême, at the beginning of the 19th century thought it came from an obscure verb, magnonner, meaning to stir – and stir – and stir.*

*So long as all ingredients and utensils are at warm-room temperature, and you begin slowly, your mayonnaise will never curdle. If it does, on account of cold or impatience, put a tablespoon of mustard into a clean basin, and add the curdled mixture slowly: or use another egg yolk instead of mustard.*

METHOD Beat the egg yolks well in a mortar, plus half the mustard if used, and a teaspoonful of vinegar or lemon juice. Start adding the olive oil, *drop by drop*. When the mixture begins to thicken properly, the oil can be added in a steadier stream. Finally flavour with remaining mustard and vinegar or lemon juice, salt and pepper.

SAUCE MALTAISE See page 38.

### Ingredients

*2 large egg yolks*
*½ pint olive or corn oil*
*1-2 tablespoons* wine *vinegar or lemon juice*
*Up to 1 tablespoon French mustard (optional)*
*Salt, pepper*

## SAUCE HOLLANDAISE

*This is really a French sauce in spite of its name, which may be a genuflection to the excellence of Holland in matters of dairy produce. Remember that this sauce is a hot mayonnaise – go cautiously with the heat and the butter. If it curdles, put an egg yolk into a clean basin and add the spoilt mixture drop by drop until it regains its aplomb. When this sauce has to stand about in hot kitchens, it is the habit to add a tablespoon of thick Béchamel or velouté at the beginning. To me this spoils the rich light texture, but I pass on the hint.*

METHOD Boil first three ingredients until reduced to just over a tablespoon of liquid. Strain into a basin. When cool beat in the yolks, stand over a pan of very hot but not boiling water, on a low heat. Stir in the butter bit by bit (use a wooden spoon, as with mayonnaise). When the sauce is thick, correct the seasoning with salt and lemon juice. Serve with vegetables and fish.

MALTAISE See *asparagus sauce maltaise* recipe on page 38.

BÉARNAISE Boil down 1 chopped shallot, 2 tablespoons tarragon and chervil, 4 tablespoons tarragon vinegar and some black

### Ingredients

*3 tablespoons white wine vinegar*
*2 tablespoons water*
*10 white peppercorns*
*3 large egg yolks*
*6-8 ounces unsalted butter, cut in 12 pieces*
*Salt, lemon juice to taste*

# France

pepper, until 2 tablespoons of liquid are left. Complete as for hollandaise. Strain into sauce boat and add chopped tarragon and chervil: for steak and *noisettes* of lamb with courgettes.

## SAUCE BERCY

*A sauce of concentrated and piquant flavour, served in small quantities with grilled steak or liver. If juices from foil-baking are added instead of meat essence, it makes an excellent sauce with fish.*

**Ingredients**
4 shallots, chopped, or 4 tablespoons chopped onion
6 ounces white wine
¼ pint meat jelly, or essence from roasting meat, or concentrated fish stock
1 tablespoon butter
Lemon juice to taste
Chopped parsley

METHOD Put shallots and wine into a small pan and boil until there is about 4 or 5 tablespoons of liquid left. Stir in the jelly, essence or stock. Season. Just before serving stir in the butter so that it melts into the sauce but does not cook, a squeeze of lemon juice to taste, and about one teaspoon chopped parsley.

## VINAIGRETTE OR FRENCH DRESSING

*Do not trust cookery books which tell you that the proportion of vinegar to oil should be 1 to 3. The result is far too strong. All the French cooks I have ever known used 5 or 6 parts of oil to 1 part of vinegar, always wine vinegar. Lemon juice can be substituted but not malt vinegar which is far too brutish in flavour. Variation of seasoning is infinite.*

**Ingredients**
1 tablespoon wine vinegar
1 heaped teaspoon French mustard
1 crushed clove garlic
About ¼ teaspoon sugar
Salt, pepper
5-6 tablespoons oil, preferably olive

METHOD Make a thickish paste with the first five ingredients. Beat in the oil gradually.

Finely chopped onion may be added, and a good handful of appropriate herbs. Gherkins and capers give extra piquancy.

FOR GREEN SALAD Mix the vinaigrette in a salad bowl. Lay the servers on top of it, crossed, to make a support for the washed and dried lettuce or other salad greens. Turn the salad carefully at table, so that every leaf is lightly coated with dressing. Never do this in advance or the salad will become slimy.

## RILLETTES AND RILLONS (pork)
(cold dishes)
*Two of the most delicious products sold in the cooked pork shops, or* charcuteries. *Rillettes are a kind of potted pork, thready, unctuous and well-spiced:* rillons *are chunks of pork belly cooked to a golden brown.*

METHOD Remove skin from pork, but not the bones. Cut half into 2-inch squares: these are the *rillons*. Cut the rest into strips about 2 inches long and ½ inch across – the *rillettes*. Using a heavy iron pot for preference, melt the lard, with the thyme and cloves of garlic. Cook for a moment or two, then put in all the pork, the water, salt and spices. Cover and leave for 4 hours over a low flame. Or put into a low oven, so that it simmers gently.

After 4 hours, remove the *rillettes* to a colander set over a basin. Turn up the heat under the pot so that the *rillons* can brown all over. Eat them warm, if you like, with apple sauce and mashed potatoes, or cold with French mustard and salad.

Now for the *rillettes*. Tear them apart with a couple of forks, to reduce them to a thready mass. *Do not put them through the mincer.* Discard bones. Put the *rillettes* into a clean pan, add more salt and spice if this seems a good idea, and a little of the fat from the meat juices which have fallen through the colander. Bring to the boil and put into sterilised stoneware pots or glass bottling jars. If they are not being eaten straightaway, cover them with a layer of melted lard. They keep well.

*Note*: boned wild rabbit, goose and hare are sometimes included with the pork – you then have *rillettes de lapin de garenne, d'oie,* or *de lièvre.* But there should be at least half the total weight of pork belly to provide the necessary fatness.

**Ingredients**

*4-5 pounds pork belly*
*2 ounces lard*
*4 cloves garlic*
*2 sprigs thyme*
*¼ pint water*
*2 ounces salt*
*1 teaspoon freshly ground black pepper*
*¼ teaspoon each - or more - of nutmeg, powdered cloves and cinnamon*

## CHICKEN LIVER PATÉ FROM CHAGNY
## PATÉ DE CHAGNY
(cold dish)

*4-6 helpings*

*A particularly simple and delicious pâté, from the Hotel Lameloise at Chagny in Burgundy. Two things to remember when making any pâté – too much* lean *bacon can be a disaster from a flavour point of view, and a fair proportion of pork fat in one form or another is essential.*

METHOD Remove any stringy bits or greenish-looking gall bladders from the chicken liver, then chop roughly or reduce to a purée in a moulinette or liquidiser. Mix with sausages (discard skins), egg, herbs, seasonings and alcohol. Put into a pint terrine, or two smaller ones: arrange bay leaf and strips of fat on top. Stand in pan of boiling water and bake for 45 minutes in a fairly hot oven. Best kept for 2 days before eating, for the flavours to develop.

**Ingredients**

*½ pound chicken livers*
*6 ounces sausages*
*1 egg*
*About ¼ teaspoon salt*
*Plenty of freshly ground black pepper*
*Good pinch thyme and marjoram*
*1 tablespoon brandy*
*2-3 tablespoons Madeira or brown sherry*
*Bay leaf*
*Strips of fat from pork or bacon*

**GM 6 400°F**
**200°C**

# France

## ANCHOVIES
## L'ANCHOÏADE

*Anchoïade is the name given to a variety of sauces from southern France, which have anchovies as their predominant flavour. Good delicatessens often sell salted anchovies by number or weight: they have to be soaked for an hour or two, then filletted, the flavour is very good – worth the small amount of trouble required.*

*A simple anchoïade can be made by liquidising half a dozen or so anchovy fillets with an olive-oil vinaigrette (for tomato salads, or mixtures of rice, tunny fish, hard-boiled eggs etc.). Anchovies pounded with egg yolks before making a mayonnaise produce a deliciously rich sauce for serving with cold fish such as salt cod, or with hard-boiled eggs, or with soaked and boiled haricot beans served warm.*

*Here, though, is the finest version of all, based on a recipe from a great collection of regional dishes made by Count Austin de Croze in the 1920s. It's something special, but go carefully with the orange-flower water as it is a most powerful substance.*

### Ingredients

2 ounces green herbs, chopped
(parsley, chives etc.)
1 6-inch stalk green fennel,
chopped
2 cloves garlic, chopped
3 dried figs, chopped
1 small sweet red pepper,
seeded
12 blanched almonds
24 anchovy fillets in oil (1½
tins approx.)
12 salted anchovies, soaked,
boned
6 tablespoons fruity olive oil
Lemon juice
1½ teaspoons orange-flower
water (from chemist)
6 finger rolls, or 12 bridge
rolls
8 ounces black olives

**GM 7 425°F
220°C**

METHOD Mix first five ingredients. Pound together the next four, adding about half the oil or a little more. Combine the two mixtures. Flavour with lemon juice, then orange-flower water to taste. Split open the rolls, removing a little of the crumb. Divide the anchoiade between them, spreading it on the top cut side. Brush the bottom cut side with the remaining oil, and put together again. Place on a baking sheet. Brush tops with olive oil. Leave in a hot oven for 5 minutes. Serve immediately surrounded with the black olives.

An outstanding hors d'oeuvre, piquant, but not too filling. The mixture can be made very rapidly in a liquidiser: drop the hard items on to the whirling blades first, moistening as you go with olive oil – a little more may be needed. Stop before the mixture is totally emulsified; there should be plenty of small bits and pieces in it. The sauce can be prepared well in advance, the day before if you like. Brush rolls with oil and heat at the last minute.

## CHEESE POTATOES
## GRATIN DAUPHINOIS

*A lovely filling dish, to be recommended especially to those who can buy or grow waxy potatoes – fir apple, Kipfler, and so on. Good new potatoes can be used instead.*

### Ingredients

1 pound potatoes
1 clove garlic, split
Salt, pepper, nutmeg
2-3 ounces butter
3 ounces grated cheese,
preferably Gruyère and

METHOD Peel and slice the potatoes thinly into a bowl of water. Use a mandoline, or the cucumber blade of a grater. Grease a gratin dish with a butter paper, and rub it over thoroughly with the cut side of the garlic. Drain and dry the potatoes in a cloth, and arrange them in even layers in the dish, seasoning each one with salt, pepper, nutmeg, and some dabs of butter and a little cheese. Finish with a good even layer of cheese. Mix cream with water and pour over the whole thing. Bake in a fairly warm oven until the potatoes are cooked – an hour at least. Brown under the grill, or turn up the oven high for the last 10 minutes of cooking time. Serve hot and bubbling.

*Parmesan mixed*
*½ pint double cream*
*4 tablespoons water*

**GM 2-3 300°–325°F**
**155°–170°C**

## VEGETABLE STEW
## RATATOUILLE À LA NIÇOISE

*6 helpings*

*Ratatouille is one of those helpful dishes, the ingredients of which can be adjusted to availability or your pocket. Serve it hot or cold, on its own or with lamb, veal, steaks and grilled chops. The name is a Provençal word, meaning a stew. The one thing to avoid is wateriness. Olive oil is essential.*

METHOD Slice courgettes and aubergines: arrange in a colander, sprinkle with salt and leave for an hour to drain. Peel and chop tomatoes roughly. Remove stalk and seeds from peppers, cut into strips. Peel and slice onions thinly.

In the olive oil, melt the garlic and anchovy, crushing them

*Ingredients*
*1 pound courgettes*
*1 pound aubergines*
*1 pound tomatoes*
*2-3 sweet peppers*
*2-3 large onions*
*4 tablespoons olive oil*
*2 cloves garlic, chopped*
*2 anchovy fillets (optional)*
*Salt, pepper*
*A few coriander seeds*
*Fresh basil or parsley*

*Ratatouille*
*à la Niçoise.*

with a wooden spoon. Add the onion. As it softens (without browning), add the dried aubergines and peppers. Cover and simmer for 20 minutes. Put in tomatoes and courgettes. Season with salt, pepper and coriander. Cook steadily until all wateriness has disappeared – up to 50 minutes. This is best done without a lid on the pan. Serve hot or cold, sprinkled with chopped basil or parsley.

*Note*: Sugar or tomato concentrate may be necessary to improve the flavour of the tomatoes.

## ASPARAGUS WITH SAUCE MALTAISE
## ASPERGES SAUCE MALTAISE

*4 helpings*

*Malta being famous for its oranges, maltaise in French cookery has come to mean 'flavoured with oranges', blood oranges for preference.*

**Ingredients**
*2 pounds asparagus*
*1 pound new potatoes (optional)*
Either *hollandaise sauce* or *mayonnaise sauce*
*Plus 1 large blood or Seville orange*

METHOD Peel asparagus stalks with potato peeler if necessary. Trim 2 inches off the ends, and tie the rest into four bundles. Scrape the potatoes. Put a large pan of salted water on to heat, and when boiling stand the bunches of asparagus up in it, trimmed end down. Tuck asparagus trimmings round them, with the potatoes. Drain when cooked. Keep water, potatoes and asparagus trimmings to make soup for another meal. Arrange the asparagus on a serving dish. If you are eating them hot, have ready a *hollandaise* sauce which has been flavoured finally with the grated rind and juice of the orange. When eaten cold, serve with *mayonnaise*, flavoured finally with the grated rind and juice of an orange.

## WATER-CRESS AND WALNUT SALAD
## SALADE DE CRESSON AUX NOIX

*4-6 helpings*

*Walnut trees are one of the happiest features of the French landscape from Burgundy southwards. The first fresh juicy ones are a great treat. One eats them with bread hot from the baker's oven, with unsalted butter, coarse salt and a glass of the new cloudy wine. Pounded with garlic, diluted with stock they make an excellent soup.*

**Ingredients**
*1 bunch water-cress*
*12-16 walnuts, shelled*
*2 ounces Gruyère or other cheese, diced*
*1 large crisp eating apple, cored, diced*
*2 shallots or small onions, chopped*
*1 thick slice ham (optional), diced*
*2-3 hard-boiled eggs, quartered*
*Vinaigrette with extra mustard*

METHOD Wash and pick over watercress. Put into a shallow dish. Break walnut kernels into pieces; mix with cheese, apple, shallots and ham if used. Put on top of cress with egg quarters. Pour over *vinaigrette* just before serving.

## CARROT SALAD
## CAROTTES RAPÉES

*This salad is so simple to make and so good and refreshing to eat. Serve it on a brilliant pink dish, scattered with fresh green herbs and it makes a most elegant course on its own. Incidentally, old carrots have more flavour than young ones, as well as being cheaper.*

METHOD Grate carrots finely into a pudding basin (or coarsely, if you prefer). Mix in shallot or onion, vinaigrette and extra mustard to taste. Fold in a couple of tablespoons of chopped herbs – the aniseed flavours of fennel or tarragon go well with carrot, and give an extra character to the salad. Chill until required. Drain off surplus liquid, and serve carrots with some freshly chopped herbs on top.

*Ingredients*
*1 medium carrot per person, peeled*
*½ shallot or small onion, per person, chopped*
*Vinaigrette*
*Extra French mustard*
*Chopped parsley and chives*
*Or, chopped fennel and parsley*
*Or, chopped tarragon and parsley*

## LEEK AND POTATO SOUP
## POTAGE À LA BONNE FEMME

*4-6 helpings*

*Potage bonne femme is a favourite choice with French families to begin their light evening meal. This is mainly because the ingredients are always to hand (leeks are sold throughout the summer – in northern France, at any rate). When preparing the leeks, discard the coarse dark leaves, using only the white and pale green part.*

METHOD Put leek, onion and butter into a pan. Stew slowly, covered, for about 10 minutes, shaking the pan from time to time so that the vegetables neither brown nor stick. Add potatoes, water and seasoning. When vegetables are cooked, set aside a few slices of leek and potato, and liquidise the rest. Bring to desired consistency with milk; add cream or a nice knob of butter, and reheat without boiling, with the reserved slices of potato and leek. Correct seasoning. *Croûtons* can be served with this soup.

*Ingredients*
*4 medium leeks, sliced*
*1 medium onion, chopped*
*2 ounces butter*
*½-¼ pound potatoes, sliced*
*1 pint water*
*Salt, pepper*
*Up to 1 pint milk*
*¼ pint single cream, or extra butter*

## CRÈME VICHYSSOISE GLACÉE

*8 helpings*

*A famous and elegant soup invented by a French chef, Louis Diat, while he was working at the Ritz-Carlton in New York. He diluted his* bonne femme *soup with plenty of cream, chilled it well and served it with a sprinkling of chopped chives instead of the slices of potato and leek.*

## WATERCRESS SOUP
## SOUPE AU CRESSON DE LA FONTAINE

*4-6 helpings*

*Substitute a large bunch of watercress for half the leeks in the* bonne femme *recipe. Chop the stalks roughly and cook in with the soup. Add the leaves when liquidizing the soup, or chop them finely and add when reheating it.*

# France

**4-6 helpings**  
## SORREL SOUP
## POTAGE SANTÉ

Potage sante *means, literally, health soup and refers to the
refreshing flavour of sorrel, referred to in the following
recipe. In spring when the first leaves appear, it tastes most
reviving after winter's heavy food.*

METHOD To the *bonne femme* soup above, add, finally, a large
handful of sorrel which has been cut in strips – use scissors – and
melted to a purée in 2 ounces of butter. Serve with toast rather
than croûtons.

## CUCUMBER AND SORREL SOUP IN THE RUSSIAN STYLE
## POTAGE D'OSEILLE À LA RUSSE

*4-6 helpings*

*Few gardens in France are without a patch of sorrel. It's the cook's great standby. A handful melted in butter gives a delicious sharp finish to plain vegetable soups. A larger quantity, extended with cream, stock or butter, makes a quick sauce for veal, eggs, salmon, mackerel and other fish.*

*If you have none to hand, spinach and lemon juice may be used instead.*

METHOD Wash and chop sorrel (or spinach). Stir over moderate heat – no added liquid – until reduced to a purée. When cold, add other ingredients in given order. Pour into bowls and serve chilled.

**Ingredients**
½ *pound sorrel (or spinach)*
7 *ounces single cream, or half single half double*
2 *pots natural yoghurt*
¾ *pint cold consommé or beef stock*
½ *pound cucumber, seeded and chopped*
3 *hard-boiled eggs, chopped*
*Chopped chives*
*Chopped fennel leaves or tarragon*
*Salt, pepper (lemon juice) to taste*

## FRENCH ONION SOUP
## SOUPE À L'OIGNON

*4-6 helpings*

*When Les Halles was still the belly of Paris, the great market of the capital, small restaurants around the central buildings used to serve this reviving soup at all hours of the night. The success of this soup depends on the stock and the brandy.*

METHOD Slice the onions very thinly. Cook without browning them in the butter. Add stock, and simmer for 45 minutes. Just before serving, add the brandy. Toast the bread towards the end of the cooking time, put grated Gruyère cheese on it and float on the soup.

*Note*: The finished bowl of soup can also be placed under the grill for the cheese to brown – this is a most excellent way of finishing it.

**Ingredients**
1 *pound onions*
2 *ounces butter*
2½-3 *pints beef stock*
*Up to 4 ounces cognac*
8-12 *slices of French bread*
4-6 *ounces grated Gruyère cheese*

# France

### FISH SOUP
6 helpings    ### COTRIADE

*Cotriade is the fish soup of Brittany, and, with the chaudrees of the Biscayan coast, the ancestor of American chowders (*chaudree *and* chowder *derive from* chaudiere, *an iron cauldron). You can eat the soup as it is, or you can remove the fish and potato and eat them as the main course with plenty of good bread and butter.*

*Ingredients*
*2 tablespoons lard*
*2 large onions, chopped*
*3 cloves garlic, chopped*
*2 pounds potatoes, peeled and quartered*
*Chervil, parsley, chives in quantity*
*Fish: 2 mackerel*
*3 gurnard*
*8 ounces conger eel*
*2 whiting*
*1 small bream*
*or, a choice of these*

METHOD Melt the lard and cook onions and garlic in it gently for 10 minutes, without browning. Add potatoes and stir up well, then the herbs. Cover generously with water. Season. Cut the cleaned fish into sizeable chunks, and add them to the pot when the potatoes are almost cooked: they will need about 5 minutes cooking – remember that they will continue to cook in the heat of the soup as you dish it up, so even quite large chunks should need no more than 8 minutes. Peeled and chopped tomatoes make a good addition.

### THE FRENCH WAY OF BAKING FISH

*An excellently simple recipe which can be adapted to most whole fish, whether from sweet or salt water. The ingredients can be varied according to what you have in the house or garden. Several small fish can of course be baked together: scale and clean them first, season the cavities and fill with a herb stuffing if you like, but leave the heads on.*

*Choose an ovenproof dish in which the fish or fishes will lie in one layer, as closely fitting as possible. Butter the dish generously, and cover the base with finely chopped onion, shallot, mushrooms and green herbs. If the fish are less than $1\frac{1}{2}$ lbs in weight, sweat the onion etc in butter separately first, or they won't have time to cook through. Lay the fish on top of the vegetables (don't forget the seasoning), brush it or them with butter and put into a hot oven, for 10 minutes. Then pour on a glass of dry white wine, or a little more for a very large fish: there should be enough to come $\frac{1}{2}$ of the way up it. Lower the heat to fairly hot, and leave until cooked. Serve with lemon quarters, and boiled new potatoes, or good bread and butter.*

GM 6 400°F
200°C
reducing to
GM 5 375°F
190°C

*If you like, pour a glass of double cream over the fish just before serving. Or sprinkle some breadcrumbs on top and flash under a very hot grill.*

### RED MULLET IN THE ORIENTAL STYLE
6 helpings    ### ROUGET-BARBET À L'ORIENTALE

*Red mullet are among the best fish in the sea. The liver is a great delicacy. They vary in size: larger mullet can be split in half when cooked (discard the backbone), in which case 3 would be enough.*

# France

METHOD Scale and clean the mullet, preserving the liver carefully. Put tomatoes into a pan with two-thirds of the olive oil and the garlic. As they begin to boil down, add wine, saffron, herbs, seeds and seasoning. Cook for 20 minutes steadily, uncovered, so that you end up with a stew or substantial sauce. Correct seasoning to taste. Meanwhile turn mullet in seasoned flour and fry until golden brown and cooked in the remaining oil about 4-5 minutes a side. Put them into a lightly oiled baking dish and pour over the tomato mixture. Bake in a very hot oven for 5 minutes. Leave to cool. Serve chilled, decorated with slices of lemon.

## Ingredients
*6 mullet*
*2 pounds tomatoes, peeled*
*¼ pint olive oil*
*1 clove garlic, chopped*
*¼ pint dry white wine*
*Pinch of saffron filaments*
*Bouquet garni*
*Chopped fennel leaves or*
  *aniseed*
*¼ teaspoon coriander seeds,*
  *crushed*
*Salt, pepper, sugar*
*Seasoned flour*
*1 lemon*

**GM 8 450°F**
**230°C**

# France

## SOLE OR TROUT IN THE MILLER'S WIFE'S STYLE
## SOLE OU TRUITE À LA MEUNIÈRE

*This recipe is simple enough, apart from one detail essential to its success, which is often overlooked. The butter in which the fish is fried must first be clarified or it will burn and give the sole or trout an unappetising appearance and flavour. Some people add oil to the butter instead, which does prevent it catching at its usual low temperature, but this dilutes the beautiful flavour.*

METHOD Ask the fishmonger to clean the fish, and to skin the sole if used. Melt half the butter in a small pan. When it boils, pour it into the frying pan through a sieve lined with a piece of damp muslin or cheese cloth – all the white salty bits which cause butter to burn quickly will be left behind.

Turn the fish in seasoned flour and cook on both sides until golden brown. Remove to a serving dish, wipe out the pan with kitchen paper, and melt the remaining unclarified butter until it foams. Pour it over the fish, swill the pan round with vinegar and pour that on too. Serve garnished with parsley and the lemon.

*Ingredients
per person*

*Sole or trout
1 sole or trout, 8-10 ounces
2½ ounces butter
Wine vinegar
Chopped parsley
Lemon quarter*

## SALT COD
## BRANDADE DE MORUE

*6-8 helpings*

*Salt cod from northern Europe is very popular in the Mediterranean, no doubt because it has no need of refrigeration. Soak for 48 hours, changing the water three times. Cut into six pieces, cover with water in a saucepan and bring slowly to the simmer: when the bones begin to part easily from the flesh, pour off the water and put the cod flakes and skin into a flameproof pot. You will also need the ingredients listed.*

METHOD Set the pot over a moderate heat. Pour in a spoonful or two of the oil, then of the cream or milk, and crush the cod with a wooden spoon. Add the garlic as you do this. Continue to add the rest of the oil and cream until you have a thick creamy purée: it should be very hot but never anywhere near boiling point. Season to taste, turn into a dish and garnish with the fried bread; one corner of each triangle should be dipped into the brandade, then into parsley, and the opposite corner should finally be pushed into the brandade.

Any left over can be reheated later, and used as a basis for poached or mollet eggs.

*Ingredients

1 salt cod, about 2-3 pounds
¾ pint olive oil, warmed
½ pint single cream, or milk
  plus 2 ounces butter, warmed
Large clove garlic, crushed
Salt, pepper, lemon juice
2 tablespoons chopped parsley
18 triangles of bread, fried in
  olive oil*

## SCALLOPS IN A CREAM AND GIN SAUCE
## COQUILLES ST-JACQUES FLAMBÉES 'GORDON'

*2 helpings*

*This dish is typical of Normandy cooking in its method; it can be adapted to other firm fish such as turbot or lobster.*

METHOD Roll out puff pastry and line two deep scallops shells. Prick with a fork and bake blind. Small patty pans can be used instead of scallop shells, or you can dispense with pastry

45

# France

## Ingredients

Puff pastry (optional: see method)
6-8 scallops
Seasoned flour
4 tablespoons butter
1 tablespoon oil
4-5 ounces double cream
4 tablespoons Gordon's gin
Salt, pepper, lemon juice
Chopped parsley

4-6 helpings

altogether and use two ramekins.

Slice scallops across into two discs each. Turn in flour and cook in the butter and oil. Meanwhile heat cream and reduce a little by boiling. When scallops are cooked, flame with the gin. Add salt, pepper and boiling cream. Cook for a few seconds, stirring the scallops about, then sharpen with a little lemon juice.

Divide scallops between pastry shells or pots, pour over the sauce, sprinkle with parsley and serve very hot.

## CRAB MONTECARLO
## CRABE À LA MONÉGASQUE

*A rather elaborate presentation of crab, but simple to prepare.*

## Ingredients

2 medium crabs;
Or 1 2-pound crab, plus a tin of crab meat
2 hard-boiled eggs
3 large potatoes, boiled in their skins
1 tin of French petits pois
4 gherkins
¼ pint mayonnaise
1 lettuce
2 tomatoes, peeled

METHOD Empty out the flesh of the crab(s), from the body and small claws, leaving the two large claws intact. Mix the crab meat in a large basin, plus the tinned crab if used. Fork the eggs into crumbs, dice the potatoes after skinning them, and drain the *petits pois*. Add them to the crab, with two of the gherkins, chopped fairly small. Bind the mixture with about half the

*mayonnaise* and put into the cleaned out crab shell(s). Make a bed of lettuce on a serving dish. Put the crab(s) on top, together with the large claws, which should be carefully cracked so as not to spoil their shape. Decorate with the tomatoes, cut in halves across, and the remaining gherkins and *mayonnaise*.

## ROAST VEAL WITH CREAM AND MUSHROOM SAUCE
## ROTI DE VEAU À LA CRÈME

*6 helpings*

*Veal is not a cheap meat, especially veal of a proper age (too-young veal is sold by some butchers; it looks whitish and puffy with air, so avoid it). Serve it for a special occasion, with this delicious sauce.*

METHOD Ask the butcher to tie two or three long strips of pork fat along the joint (this is known as barding). Brown it with two of the onions and the walnuts in 2 ounces butter. Pour over the Madeira, season and roast in the usual way for about an hour—test by piercing with a larding needle or skewer; when the juice is colourless, the meat is done. Slice and arrange on serving dish with the juices if they are not too burnt.

Meanwhile cook mushrooms and remaining onion in 2 ounces of butter. When soft, stir in flour and complete the sauce with milk and cream in the usual *Béchamel* style. Beat egg yolks with a little sauce, then tip into the pan and stir over a low heat, *without boiling,* until thick. Correct seasoning, and pour over the veal. Serve with potatoes or rice, with a green salad to follow. No green vegetables.

### Ingredients
*3-4 pound joint of veal, boned, rolled*
*3 onions, chopped*
*20 walnut halves, chopped*
*4 ounces butter*
*Glass Madeira or brown sherry (3 ounces)*
*Salt, pepper*
*½ pound mushrooms, sliced*
*1 rounded tablespoon flour*
*¼ pint milk*
*¼ pint single cream*
*2 egg yolks*

# France

## BEST END OF NECK OF LAMB-PRINCESS STYLE
## CARRÉ D'AGNEAU À LA PRINCESSE

*6-8 helpings*

*The French regard lamb as a luxury and they are prepared to pay high prices for it. In France lamb is served slightly rare, with a choice of deliciously cooked vegetables, arranged round it like a painting. The* carré, *exactly equivalent to our best end of neck, comprises six or eight small chops, which means that you need both sides to allow two chops each for six to eight people. Ask the butcher to leave the bones fairly long, and to cut off about an inch of the fat to expose them to view.*

### Ingredients

*Two pieces best end of neck*
*One large clove garlic peeled*
*1 teaspoonful each thyme and sage*
*Salt, pepper*
*1 onion, quartered*
*½ pint beef stock*
*1 tablespoon tomato purée*
*1 glass (6 ounces) dry white wine*
*1 level tablespoonful cornflour*
*12-16 cooked asparagus tips*
*2 ounces of butter*
*Tomatoes à la provençale*

**GM 7 425°F 220°C**

METHOD Make small cuts in the meat and push slivers of the garlic into them. Mix thyme and sage and rub them into the meat. Sprinkle with salt and pepper. Protect the exposed bones with a wrapping of foil. Place on top of the onion in a small roasting pan. Roast in a hot oven for half an hour. (Add 10-15 minutes if you prefer lamb well done.)

Transfer cooked meat to a serving dish and keep warm (remove foil). Put roasting pan over the heat, and boil up until the onion caramelises, stirring with a wooden spoon: add a little of the stock if necessary. Remove or pour off surplus fat, and add to rest of the stock. Boil up vigorously, stirring the nice brown bits and pieces into the liquid. Add tomato purée and white wine. Reduce a little, then thicken with cornflour in the usual way – the sauce should be creamy but not too thick. Correct seasoning. Reheat asparagus tips in the butter and arrange over the meat. Strain some of the sauce and put the rest into a sauce boat. Add little piles of buttered French beans (*not* scarlet runners, but true French beans: in winter use deep frozen *haricots verts*), interspersed with:

## TOMATES À LA PROVENÇALE

*A most appetising way of cooking tomatoes. Try and get hold of large craggy red ones. These are often cheapest because they do not fit into the Ministry of Agriculture grading systems. Olive oil is essential.*

### Ingredients

*6-8 tomatoes*
*6-8 tablespoons of olive oil*
*2-3 cloves garlic, finely chopped*
*2-3 tablespoons parsley, chopped*
*3-4 teaspoons breadcrumbs*
*Extra olive oil or a little butter*

METHOD Cut tomatoes in two crosswise. Remove as much juice and as many seeds as you conveniently can. Fry in oil on both sides, but do not allow to collapse or lose their shape. Put in ovenproof dish, cut side up. Mix garlic and parsley and divide between the tomatoes. Sprinkle with breadcrumbs, dot with oil or butter and brown lightly under the grill or in a hot oven.

*Best end of neck of lamb – Princess style.*

## BEEF STEWED IN THE BURGUNDY STYLE
## BOEUF À LA BOURGUIGNONNE

*4-6 helpings*

*Characteristics of the Burgundy style are a red wine sauce, a garnish of little bits of bacon or* lardons, *glazed onions and fried mushrooms, plus triangles of fried bread and a sprinkling of parsley. It is one of the best ways of cooking a variety of things – eel, beef and chicken. Once you understand the method, nobody will ever complain again about being given 'stew'.*

METHOD Turn to the recipe for *coq au vin* on page 54. Substitute 2-3 pounds of stewing beef for the chicken (I always use shin because it adds a smooth, jellied texture to the sauce) and beef stock for chicken stock. Follow **method 2.**

Serve with plenty of good bread, and have a green salad to eat afterwards.

## BEEF OLIVES
## ALOUETTES SANS TÊTES

*8 helpings*

*One of those agreeable dishes which can be adjusted to your taste and resources. The French are particularly good at making the most of left-overs, and pride themselves on the deliciousness of the result. It follows that the stuffing ingredients below are a suggestion, and in no way mandatory.*

METHOD Lay slices of beef flat, spread them with mustard and seasoning. To make the stuffing, mix bacon and cooked meat. Simmer shallot and garlic in butter, and when soft add to bacon, plus all the other stuffing ingredients. Divide between beef slices. Roll each one up, turning the sides over to enclose the stuffing, and tie twice with button thread. This can be done in advance.

To prepare the sauce, brown the onion lightly in the dripping. Add all the other vegetables and stir them together to heat up slightly. Put into a large gratin dish and lay the beef olives on top. Pour stock and wine into the pan in which the onion was browned, bring to the boil and pour round the meat. Cover and put into a warm to moderate oven for 1½ hours. Remove lid or foil after half an hour, and turn the meat parcels over after one hour.

When cooked, remove the beef olives to a warm serving dish, and cut off thread. Strain cooking liquor into a pan and boil it down. Meanwhile arrange the vegetables around the meat. When the sauce has a good flavour, thicken it with the butter and flour which have been mashed together to a paste (*beurre marié*)– the paste should be stirred in in small knobs, and the liquid kept below boiling point. All the flour and butter may not be needed. Pour some of the sauce over the meat and serve the rest in a sauce boat.

Buttered *pasta* goes well with this dish, or new potatoes or potato croquettes.

### Ingredients
*18 slices topside, about 1 ounce each*
*French mustard*
*Salt, pepper*

**stuffing**
*4 ounces green bacon, chopped*
*5-6 ounces cooked chicken/ pork/ham, chopped*
*1 shallot, chopped*
*1 large clove garlic, chopped*
*2 ounces butter*
*3 ounces fresh breadcrumbs*
*1 glass brandy (2 tablespoons) or 4 tablespoons Madeira, vermouth, white wine or dry sherry*
*1 egg*
*Plenty of parsley, thyme, chives*
*Salt, pepper*

**sauce**
*1 large onion, chopped*
*1 large carrot, chopped*
*½ pound mixed vegetables according to season*
*2 ounces beef dripping*
*¾ pint beef stock*
*¼ pint red wine*
*1 tablespoon butter*
*1 tablespoon flour*
**GM 3-4 325-350°F**
**170°-180°C**

# France

## SAUSAGE CAKES
## CRÉPINETTES AUX MARRONS

*4 helpings*

*The crepine or toilette, caul or kell to an English butcher, is the fatty veil which encloses the guts of the pig. In other words the peritoneum. When softened slightly in warm water it stretches out like a beautiful piece of patterned net curtaining, and is useful for wrapping up mixtures of pork and seasonings to make faggots, or crépinettes.*

### Ingredients
*1 piece caul fat*
*1 pound high-content meat sausages*
*6-8 ounces shelled chestnuts*
*Plenty of freshly ground black pepper*
*Spices or herbs for extra flavour*

METHOD Dip the caul fat into warm water, spread it out gently on a table, and cut it with scissors into eight roughly equal squares. Discard the sausage skins and put sausage meat into a basin with the coarsely chopped chestnuts, pepper and spices or herbs to taste. Mix well but be careful not to squash the chestnut pieces, which should remain as mealy, unmistakable items in the sausagemeat. Divide into eight, and place in the centre of the squares of caul fat. Lay one on the palm of your left hand, fold over the edges to enclose the sausage meat and flatten the little cake until it's about half an inch thick. Do the same with the rest. Fry or grill and serve with buttery mashed potatoes.

*Note*: many other ways of flavouring *crépinettes* are used in France – almonds, pistachio nuts, chopped red pepper and caraway seeds, etc.

## HAM IN CREAM SAUCE
## JAMBON DU MORVAN À LA CRÈME GRATINÉ

*4-6 helpings*

*Ham reheated in a cream sauce and browned on top is a favourite Burgundian dish. This version comes from Monsieur Minot at the Cote d'Or in Saulieu, at the heart of the Morvan pig-breeding district. The best equivalent to Morvan ham would be slices of ham on the bone, a really fine quality ham.*

### Ingredients
*12 slices cooked ham*
*¼ pound mushrooms*
*1 ounce butter*
*7 ounces Chablis, or dry white wine*
*1 large onion, chopped*
*3 shallots, chopped*
*2 large tomatoes, peeled and chopped*
*½ pint double cream*
*1 ounce grated Parmesan*
*Salt, pepper*

**GM 8 450°F**
**230°C**

METHOD Arrange ham on a large, shallow ovenproof dish. Slice mushrooms, cook in butter and scatter over the top. Now make the sauce: boil wine, onion and shallots together until a tablespoon of liquid remains. Add tomatoes. Simmer steadily for 10 minutes then sieve, pressing through as much pulp as possible. Heat cream and add vegetable purée. Season and pour over the ham. Sprinkle with the cheese. Put into a very hot oven for 10 minutes to heat through thoroughly. If the top isn't brown enough, place under grill to finish. Serve with buttered rice.

# France

## PHEASANT FRANÇOIS MINOT
## FAISAN FRANÇOIS MINOT

*4-6 helpings*

*Ten years ago, François Minot was chosen by the much loved and respected Monsieur Dumaine to succeed him at one of France's most famous restaurants, the Cote d'Or at Saulieu in Burgundy. A brilliant but unenviable election. At last he feels secure in his own gifts, and introduces recipes of his invention into the menu.*

**Ingredients**

*1 fat hen pheasant, properly hung*
*Stuffing*
*1 Cox's Orange Pippin, peeled, cored and diced*
*Peel 1 orange and 1 lemon, cut into matchstick strips*
*4 chipolata sausages*
*Pheasant liver*
*A little butter*
*2 ounces cooked rice*
*Salt, pepper*
*Gravy*
*1 glass Madeira*

**GM 7 425°F 220°C**

METHOD Season the pheasant. Put the apple into a basin. Boil peel strips in water for 2 minutes, drain and add to apple. Twist or tie chipolata sausages into eight small ones: fry with liver in a little butter. Add to basin. Mix in cooked rice and season. Stuff pheasant, and roast in a hot oven for 45-60 minutes. Cut into four or carve for six: arrange on dish with stuffing in the middle. Stir Madeira into roasting juices, pour over pheasant when boiling hard and serve immediately.

## DUCK WITH ORANGE
## CANETON À LA BIGARADE

*4 helpings*

*A bigarade is a bitter orange, sometimes called a Seville orange, and this is a clue to the flavour. Out of season – but did you know that Seville oranges store well in a home freezer? French cooks compensate for the sweetness of other oranges by adding lemon juice or wine vinegar, and a little bitter orange liqueur such as Curaçao.*

**Ingredients**

*1 duck*
*2 sweet oranges*
*Water-cress*
*Sauce bigarade:*
*1 tablespoon butter*
*1 heaped tablespoon flour*
*¾ pint duck giblet stock*
*2 Seville oranges, or 2 sweet oranges and 1 lemon*
*4 teaspoons sugar*
*3 ounces dry white vermouth*
*Salt, pepper*
*Duck liver (optional)*

METHOD Roast duck in the usual way. Remove peel and pith of the 2 sweet oranges with a sharp knife, cut into slices and set aside. To make the sauce, melt butter, stir in flour, cook for 2 minutes then moisten with stock. Simmer 20 minutes. Take peel off the oranges (and lemon), cut into matchstick shreds and blanch in boiling water for 4 minutes, then strain. Flavour the sauce with orange (and lemon) juice to taste, the vermouth, sugar and seasonings. Pound a little blanched peel with the liver if used, and add to sauce just before serving with the rest of the peel. Pour fat from duck cooking juices, and heat the orange slices in them. Arrange round duck on very hot serving dish with the watercress and add the juices to the sauce. Pour sauce into sauceboat. Have all plates and dishes really hot.

## GOOSE, DUCK OR TURKEY NECK SAUSAGE
## COU D'OIE, DE CANARD OU DE DINDE FARCI

*4 helpings*

*Always buy a goose, duck or turkey with the head on: then you can make this appetising sausage. Using a very sharp knife or pair of scissors, cut the skin right round as close as*

52

*possible to the beak of the bird at one end, and to the breast of the bird at the other. Slit the skin straight up the centre, so that you can remove an uneven rectangle of fatty skin from the neck. Lay it skin side down on a board.*

**Ingredients**

*8-12 ounces high-meat content sausages*
*The liver of the bird*
*Salt, pepper*
*Chopped parsley and chives*
*Ground cinnamon, nutmeg, cloves*
*Chopped almonds or pistachio nuts*

METHOD Remove the skin from the sausages. Cut away the gall bladder and any greenish-yellow bits from the liver. Season the sausage meat according to your taste, fancy and resources, and lay it out on the poultry skin, leaving a small free margin all round. Lay the liver down the centre and bring the sausage meat round to enclose it. Sew up the skin round everything to make a bumpy sausage. Simmer in stock for 30 minutes, leave to cool in the liquid and serve, chilled, in thin slices as an hors d'oeuvre, or part of one.

*4-6 helpings*

## COQ AU VIN (chicken)

*The numerous variations of the classic* coq au vin *depend not so much on different ingredients, but on the method of cooking them. The key is the age of the chicken. A farmyard cockerel is the obvious choice, but a boiling fowl of good quality (not a retired egg-laying machine) gives an even better result if cooked by method 2.*

**Ingredients**

*1 bird, 3-4 pounds weight, jointed*
*Seasoned flour*
*4 ounces butter*
*3 onions, chopped*
*3 cloves garlic, chopped*
*1 glass brandy*
*¾ pint red wine, heated*
*Up to ¾ pint chicken stock, heated*
*Bouquet garni*
*8 ounce piece salt pork, or smoked or green streaky bacon, cut into thick strips*
*18 pickling onions*
*½ pound small button mushrooms*
*Salt, pepper, chopped parsley*
*18 triangles of fried bread*

METHOD 1, FOR ROASTING BIRD. Turn chicken pieces in seasoned flour. Brown lightly in the butter. Remove to a plate, and put *all* vegetables and garlic, plus bacon or pork, into the pan. When they are a nice colour, put back the chicken. Flame it with brandy, and pour in wine with enough chicken stock, if necessary, to cover the bird. Simmer uncovered until cooked. Correct seasoning. If the sauce seems watery, pour it into another pan and reduce hard by boiling. Transfer to a serving dish, sprinkle with parsley and tuck triangles of fried bread round the edge.

METHOD 2, FOR BOILING FOWL. A boiler needs long, slow cooking: but the small vegetables must keep their character. So this is what you do: brown the floured chicken in half the butter together with garlic and *chopped* onion. Flame with brandy, add wine and stock as above, and leave to simmer, covered, until cooked. Meanwhile brown the pork or bacon pieces in the rest of the butter with the pickling onions (the onions can be glazed separately if you are feeling particularly professional – put them in a pan in a single layer, cover with water, add a tablespoon each butter and sugar and boil hard until liquid is reduced to a caramelised glaze, by which time the onions will be cooked). Add the mushrooms and brown them too. Turn this garnish into the pan of chicken 10 minutes before it is to be served. Finish sauce as above.

This method produces the more elegant dish, but you pay for it with your time. On the other hand half the cooking of the bird can be done in advance. Obviously the better the wine the better the sauce, but even if you have to use cheap supermarket wine it will still taste rich and good, particularly if you add a lump or two of sugar or a tablespoon of tomato purée to help it along.

# France

## THE FRENCH WAY OF COOKING VEGETABLES

*An excellent method which I can recommend, particularly if you follow the French system of serving vegetables on their own as a separate course. It can be adapted to almost every-thing – tomatoes, and tender young peas being the most obvious exceptions. Recommended especially for celery and Florentine fennel, also for Brussels sprouts, cauliflower, new potatoes or old potatoes cut up, green beans, turnips, whole onions, frozen asparagus (fresh is better cooked in water only), peas past their first youth, carrots, parsnips, cabbage.*

*Half-fill a huge pan with water. Add a heaped teaspoon of sea salt for every 2 pints. Bring to a rolling boil. Tip in vegetables. Bring rapidly back to the boil, and cook until vegetables are two-thirds cooked, i.e. they should still be crunchy; allow 6-18 minutes according to the tenderness of the vegetable. Pour into colander, cool under the cold tap. Leave to drain for up to an hour. Your vegetables are now blanched.*

*Melt a good large knob of butter in a clean pan: 2-3 ounces. Sweat chopped garlic and onion in it, if appropriate. Add vegetables, cover and stew until cooked. Correct seasoning.*

*Some vegetables – turnips, small onions, carrots – should be sprinkled with a tablespoon of sugar towards the end; remove the lid and leave to caramelise. Other vegetables benefit from the addition of a spoonful or two of cream (double is best, but single will do) about two minutes before serving. With the butter this makes a most delicious sauce. A sprinkling of chopped parsley and chives makes an ex-quisite dish. Or blanched vegetables can be mixed with Béchamel or Mornay sauce, and put into a fairly hot oven to finish cooking.*

GM 5-6 375°-400°F
190°-200°C

## YOUNG PEAS COOKED IN THE FRENCH STYLE
## PETITS POIS À LA FRANÇAISE

*During the late Renaissance, Italian gardeners developed new varieties; peas came to be regarded as a treat. They are one of the delicacies of early summer. You may even find it difficult to buy tender young peas in the pod. To have the true* petits pois *you need to grow your own, but the recipe can be used for frozen peas with good results.*

METHOD Shell the peas if necessary. Wash and cut the lettuce into strips. Melt the butter in a saucepan, and cook the onions in it until they colour very slightly (they must not brown, but look a whitish opaque colour). Add the lettuce, then the peas and herbs. Stir in half the sugar, with plenty of pepper, a little salt and 4 tablespoons water. Cover and cook gently until done. (A couple of very young, tender carrots can be finely chopped and put in with the onions.) Pour everything into a hot dish and serve. The lettuce dissolves to a smooth liquid and gives a special texture to the sauce.

*Ingredients*

*2 pounds peas, or about*
*1 pound shelled peas*
*1 fine lettuce*
*4 ounces butter*
*½ pound tiny onions or*
*    spring onions*
*2 tablespoons chopped parsley*
*1 sprig savory, if possible*
*Up to 1 level tablespoon sugar*
*Salt, pepper*

55

# France

## CAULIFLOWER OR CHICORY IN THE POLISH STYLE
## CHOUFLEUR OU ENDIVES À LA POLONAISE

*4-6 helpings*

*The* polonaise *garnish is a most attractive one for vegetables served as a course on their own, or as a supper dish. It is normally used with cauliflower or chicory, but can be used with broccoli spears, asparagus, potatoes and so on.*

**Ingredients**
*1 fine cauliflower*
*or 8-12 heads chicory*
*4 ounces butter*
*4 hard-boiled eggs*
*2 ounces white breadcrumbs*
*Plenty of chopped parsley*

METHOD Cook vegetables in the usual way. Drain well. Break up cauliflower and fry it gently in 1 ounce of the butter, or brown the chicory lightly. Arrange on a serving dish and keep warm (put the chicory like the spokes of a wheel). Shell and fork the eggs into crumbs. Fry the breadcrumbs until golden-brown in 1½ ounces butter. Mix the egg and parsley and put over the centre of the vegetables; scatter the crumbs over the top. Melt the remaining butter and pour it foaming over the whole thing just before serving.

*Cauliflower served with a polonaise garnish.*

## CREAM CHEESE MOUSSE
## COEUR À LA CRÈME

*4-6 helpings*

*Fresh curd cheese, enriched with cream and lightened with stiffly beaten egg white, is often served with fresh fruit such as strawberries. In winter time it comes with apricot jam and some tuiles amandes. Here is a recipe for cream cheese mousse, which is eaten in much the same way in winter time, chopped ginger in syrup goes well with it; in summer raspberries, strawberries or sliced peaches, plus some cream.*

**Ingredients**
*½ pound low fat cottage cheese*
*2 egg yolks*
*2 ounces sugar*
*½ ounce packet gelatine*
*6 tablespoons very hot water*
*4 ounces each double and single cream*

METHOD Sieve the cream cheese, beat in yolks and sugar. Dissolve gelatine in water and add that. (The simplest way to do all this is to put everything into a liquidiser, and whirl at top speed for a few seconds.) Whip the creams together, and fold into the cheese mixture. Pour into little heart moulds, which have been brushed thinly with tasteless cooking oil; or into 1 larger mould. Leave to set. Serve chilled.

# France

**6-8 helpings**    **SOUFFLÉ GLACÉ GRAND MARNIER**

*Soufflés glacés are a great feature of French restaurants. Sometimes they are flavoured with lemon and decorated with candied violets, but the favourite is probably this orange-flavoured recipe.*

METHOD Dissolve sugar and cold water together over a low heat.

When boiling, raise heat and cook to the soft ball stage. Meanwhile melt gelatine in hot water. Pour sugar quickly onto the egg yolks, then the gelatine, stirring hard as you do so. Beat (preferably with an electric whisk) until the mixture is cold and fluffy. Beat cream until it holds its shape and fold that into the egg mixture with lemon juice and enough Grand Marnier to give a pleasant flavour. If you are short on liqueur, use orange juice as well. Whisk egg whites until firm and fold them in gently just before the mixture sets. Pour into a collared, 1-pint soufflé dish. When well chilled and firm, press macaroon crumbs into the sides and top of the mousse.

*Ingredients*
*8 ounces sugar*
*4 tablespoons cold water*
*2½-ounce packet gelatine*
*6 tablespoons very hot water*
*7 egg yolks*
*½ pint double cream*
*Juice of 1 lemon*
*2-3 liqueur glasses Grand Marnier cordon rouge*
*7 egg whites*
*2 macaroons, crushed*

## CHOCOLATE MOUSSE WITH ALMONDS
## MARQUISE AU CHOCOLAT

*8 helpings*

*There are many recipes for cakes called Marquise in French, and they vary enormously in everything except the inclusion of chocolate. This version is a personal favourite that makes a change from the classic chocolate mousse, and is still simple to make.*

METHOD Melt the chocolate over boiling water in the usual way. When soft stir in butter, bit by bit, and sugar. Then beat in the yolks one by one. Remove from the heat and fold in the almonds or macaroon crumbs. Whisk egg whites with a pinch of salt until very stiff. Fold into chocolate mixture, pour into a mould and chill for at least 14 hours, or more if convenient. Serve with *tuiles aux amandes*, or on its own, decorated with whipped cream.

*Ingredients*
*8 ounces Chocolat-Menier*
*6 ounces unsalted butter*
*3½ ounces icing sugar*
*5 egg yolks*
*8 ounces ground almonds or macaroon crumbs*
*5 egg whites*
*Pinch salt*

## ALMOND BISCUITS
## TUILES AUX AMANDES

*These delicate biscuits are shaped like the curved tiles of southern France – hence their name. Eat them on their own with coffee or tea, or serve them with ices, creams and stewed fruit.*

METHOD Beat sugar and egg whites together lightly. Cut almonds into fine flakes and fold them in with the flour. Melt the butter and add that.

Line baking sheets with Bakewell non-stick vegetable parchment, and put eight small teaspoons of the mixture on each one, spreading them out with a knife. If you have to bake two batches, don't worry, the mixture can stand around without coming to any harm. Give them 10 minutes in a fairly hot oven. Remove when they are golden brown at the edges, and press round a rolling pin while still hot (protect your hand with a clean cloth). They cool rapidly into an attractive curving shape.

*Ingredients*
*3½ ounces sugar*
*2 egg whites*
*Scant 3 ounces almonds, blanched*
*Generous ounce flour*
*Generous ounce butter*

**GM 6 400°F**
**200°C**

## PITHIVIERS CAKE
## GÂTEAU DE PITHIVIERS FEUILLETÉ

*Pithiviers on the east side of the Beauce, the great corn plain of France centering on Chartres, has three specialities – lark*

*pies and pâtés, pain d'épice and this most attractive-looking almond cake. The recipe still used is the same as the one given by the great chef Caréme, at the beginning of the 19th century.*

METHOD Roll out half the pastry and use to line a greased enamel or tin pie plate, about 9½ inches diameter. Alternatively put a flat circle of pastry on to a paper-lined baking sheet. Mix filling ingredients together, and place on the pastry, leaving a 1-inch rim free. Brush rim with water and lay the other half of the pastry on top. Trim and press down all round so that the two layers of pastry stick together. With a knife make 12 evenly placed nicks round the edge. Using your thumbs push up the pastry on either side of each one to form a scalloped effect. Make a hole in the centre, brush over with beaten egg and leave for 5 minutes. Now with the point of a knife, score inner scallop lines round the edge, and curving lines from the scallops to the central hole – a petal effect. Be careful not to go through the pastry.

Bake in a very hot oven for 20 minutes until the pastry is well risen. Lower the heat to fairly hot level and leave for 10 minutes until the cake is nicely browned. Take out of the oven, raise the heat back to very hot again, and while you wait for the temperature to rise dredge the Pithiviers with icing sugar. Place in the oven until the sugar melts to a rich brown glaze. Be careful not to burn it. Serve warm with a jug of single cream.

**Ingredients**
*1 pound (two packets)*
*   prepared puff pastry*
*Filling:*
*4 ounces ground almonds*
*4 ounces castor sugar*
*2 ounces melted butter*
*2 egg yolks*
*2 tablespoons double cream*
*2 tablespoons rum (optional)*

*Glaze:*
*1 small egg, beaten*
*Icing sugar*

**GM 8 450°F**
**230°C**

**reduce to**
**GM 6 400°F**
**200°C**

**raised to**
**GM 8 450°F**
**230°C**

## PARIS-BREST

*An easy but impressive cake, made simply with choux pastry and almonds, and filled with an almond-flavoured whipped cream.*

METHOD First make the pastry; bring butter and water to the boil, stirring well. Remove immediately from the heat and pour in flour and salt all at once. Mix with a wooden spoon and return to a low flame and beat until the mixture forms a soft but coherent ball of dough. Cool slightly, then beat in the eggs one at a time. The pastry will look satiny. Pipe into a ring on a baking tray lined with non-stick vegetable parchment. Put the split almonds round the top. Bake in a hot oven for 20 minutes. Remove the cake, split it here and there round the centre so that the steam can escape, and return to a moderate oven to dry out for 10 minutes.

Next, prepare the filling. First make the almond flavouring known as praline powder. Wash the almonds and split them. Melt sugar with a little water in a small pan. As it begins to brown, stir in almonds. When it's a fine toffee colour, pour on to a greased tray to cool. Pound in a mortar, or grind electrically until reduced to a powder. This keeps well in a covered jar, and is one of the finest flavourings for ice cream, butter creams and so on: I usually make it in quantity. Whip the creams together until stiff and flavour to taste with the praline powder. When the cake is cool, split it completely and fill with the almond cream. Replace top, dredge with icing sugar and serve as soon as possible.

**Ingredients**
*Choux pastry:*
*2 ounces butter*
*¼ pint water*
*2½ ounces plain flour*
*Pinch salt*
*2 eggs*
*Decoration:*
*2-3 ounces almonds, blanched,*
*   split*
*Icing sugar*
*Filling:*
*2 ounces unblanched almonds*
*3 ounces castor sugar*
*A little water*
*¼ pint double cream*
*3 ounces single cream*

**GM 7 425°F**
**220°C**
**reduce to**
**GM 4 350°F**
**180°C**

# *France*

## GÂTEAU ST HONORÉ

*St Honoré was Bishop of Amiens. One day, while he was celebrating mass, a divine hand sent down a loaf of bread. So the bakers adopted him as their patron saint. The street in Paris called the rue St Honoré used to be the place for cakes, and it was there that this one was invented at about 1879 by a pastry cook named Chiboust.*

METHOD Make choux pastry. Roll out shortcrust, cut a large circle and lay it on a baking sheet. Pipe the choux pastry round the edge to form a wall: pipe the remaining choux pastry into small balls on a separate paper-lined baking tray. Bake in a hot oven for 20 minutes. Pierce choux pastry inconspicuously for steam to escape, and return to a moderate oven for 10 minutes.

Bring sugar and water to the caramel stage. Dip each small puff into the syrup so that it acquires a cap of toffee. Dip the opposite end in and place it on the choux pastry wall – the toffee acts as glue. If you like, leave one small puff for the centre. Whip the cream, sweeten it slightly and put in the centre just before serving. Decorate with glacé fruits and toasted almonds.

### Ingredients
*Choux pastry, as above*
*4 ounces shortcrust pastry*
*¼ pound sugar*
*4 tablespoons water*
*½ pint whipping or mixed creams*
*Glacé fruits and toasted almonds (optional)*

**GM 7 425°F**
**220°C**
**reduce to**
**GM 4 350°F**
**180°C**

# Ireland

As a result of a number of sociological, historical and semi-political circumstances, Irish cookery has borrowed little from the sophistication of late 19th century recipes. It is mainly concerned with the presentation, often in the simplest way, of such fundamental ingredients as fish, meat, potatoes, flour and – surprisingly – seaweed. Few Irish recipes, for example, need or use a sauce and those that do owe less to tradition than to more recent innovation. Irish stew, for example, is one of the most nutritious dishes known and should contain not only adequate quantities of protein from mutton or kid but also carbohydrate from potatoes and onions.

Today many traditional Irish recipes such as soda bread and barm brack, eggs, bacon and ham are considered particularly suitable for breakfast or afternoon tea. For many years however, and still in country districts, these were the staples, as little else was so readily available. Regional variations were relatively few, but there was certainly a greater usage of potatoes – even in breadmaking in the west. With the possible exception of herring and mackerel, sea-fish has never been much eaten in central Ireland. On the coast there have always been such 'delicacies' as crab, lobster, mussels and prawns readily available, and country people have always enjoyed trout and salmon. Unlike Scotland, there has never been any great development of taste for 'game-birds' but the common rabbit has given its life for many a good meal.

These native recipes have been followed for centuries, without absorbing any influence from overseas. The romantic image of Ireland is still one of the 19th century, when most people lived in the remote countryside, and existed on the simple foods they could produce.

Even traditional cooking methods exist, with an extensive use in country districts of the three-legged iron pot, used for roasting, stewing and for making cakes and bread. In parts of the south and west, this is known as a 'bastable oven', and is used for the popular soda bread. The pot can be raised or lowered by a chain, and it has three short feet so that it can stand by the side of the hearth. For baking the pot is hung over a peat fire, and covered with glowing peat so that there is even heat.

Baking has always been a great tradition in Ireland, famous for its soda bread, scones, potato cakes and fruit cakes. The potato, which was such an essential item of diet, is often incorporated into cake mixtures, and this keeps the cake moist and soft.

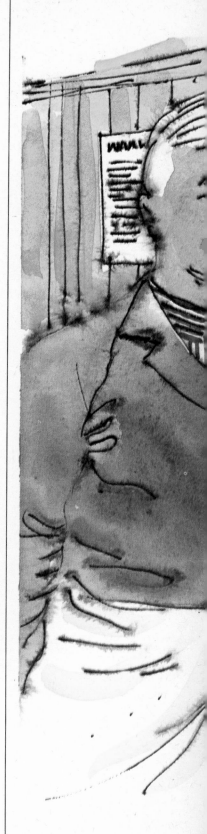

# Ireland

*12 helpings*

## HAM BOILED IN STOUT

*The best ham in Ireland comes from Limerick, where it used to be smoked with wild juniper berries. A smoked ham should be soaked in cold water for 24 hours before cooking, and a wisp of fresh hay in the cooking liquid ensures a delicious country smell in the kitchen. Often an Irish ham or piece of bacon was cooked with watercress in the water, to be served as a vegetable. A boiled ham should be finished with a coating of brown sugar and breadcrumbs, then studded with cloves.*

**Ingredients**

*1 12-pound smoked ham*
*2 pints stout*
*4 tablespoons brown sugar*
*Pinch of pepper*
*Pinch of mace*
*2 tablespoons breadcrumbs*
*Cloves*

**GM 6 400°F**
**200°C**

METHOD Soak the ham in cold water to cover for 24 hours. Drain completely and put into a large pan with the stout, half the sugar, pepper and mace, and enough cold water to cover the ham. Bring very slowly to the boil, and simmer very gently to prevent the meat becoming tough and stringy. Allow 20 to 25 minutes to the pound. For a ham to be served cold, leave the meat to cool completely in the cooking liquid, drain, and remove skin. Press breadcrumbs over the surface of the fat. For a ham to serve hot, leave the meat in the cooking liquid for 30 minutes, then remove skin. Cover with a mixture of the remaining sugar and the breadcrumbs, and stud generously with cloves. Put in a fairly hot oven for 10 minutes.

*12 helpings*

## SPICED BEEF

*This is a Christmas dish that appears in butchers' shops tied with red ribbon and decorated with holly.*

**Ingredients**

*1 6-pound boned joint of lean beef*
*3 shallots*
*4 bay leaves*
*1 teaspoon powdered cloves*
*1 teaspoon powdered mace*
*½ teaspoon crushed peppercorns*
*1 teaspoon allspice*
*½ teaspoon chopped thyme*
*3 tablespoons brown sugar*
*2 teaspoons saltpetre*
*1 pound coarse salt*
*2 tablespoons black treacle*
*3 carrots*
*3 medium onions*
*½ pint Guinness*

METHOD Chop the shallots and the bay leaves very finely. Mix the spices, thyme, sugar, saltpetre and salt. Put the meat into a large bowl and rub with the dry mixture. Turn the meat twice a day for a week, rubbing in the mixture. After two days, add the black treacle. At the end of the week, make sure the meat is tied into a neat shape. Cover with warm water and add sliced carrots and onions. Simmer gently for 4 hours. Add the Guinness and continue cooking for 1 hour. Press between two dishes with a weight on top.

*6 helpings*

## IRISH STEW

*This was originally made from kid, and later from mutton. The stew should be thick and creamy, the potatoes at the bottom having melted into the gravy.*

METHOD Make sure the meat is trimmed of fat and gristle. Keep the bones in the chops as this adds flavour. Peel the potatoes and slice one-third thinly, leaving the rest whole. Slice the onions,

# Ireland

and chop the thyme and parsley. Put the sliced potatoes into a pan, then a layer of onions and the meat. Add the herbs and remaining onion, and top with the whole potatoes. Add water and salt and pepper. Cover tightly. Cook in a warm oven for 2½ hours. The stew may be cooked on the top of the stove, very gently, for the same time.

## Ingredients

3 pounds lean neck of lamb
  chops
2 pounds potatoes
1 pound onions
Sprig of thyme
Sprig of parsley
¾ pint water
Salt and pepper

**GM 3 325°F
170°C**

*Hams of varying size can be cooked in stout.*

# Ireland

**6 helpings**

## DUBLIN CODDLE

*This is a traditional Saturday night supper dish, and has been eaten since the 18th century. It should be accompanied by fresh soda bread and glasses of stout. Sometimes sliced potatoes are added to the recipe, but this is not authentic.*

### Ingredients
1 pound onions
6 ¼-inch bacon rashers
1 pound large pork sausages
Pepper
½ pint water

METHOD Slice the onions thinly and put into a saucepan. Put in the sausages and the bacon cut into large pieces. Season with pepper (the bacon will give enough salt to the recipe) and add boiling water. Put a piece of greaseproof paper on top and then a tight lid. Simmer gently for ¾-1 hour until onions are soft. The dish may also be cooked in a cool oven for 1 hour.

**12 helpings**

## BOILED TURKEY AND CELERY SAUCE

*This way of cooking produces a succulent and juicy bird. The remaining bones and stock make excellent soup.*

### Ingredients
1 8-pound hen turkey
2 carrots
2 onions
1 bay leaf
Sprig of parsley
Sprig of thyme
Salt and pepper
Celery Sauce
1 large head celery
½ pint stock from cooking turkey
2 ounces butter
1½ ounces plain flour
⅓ pint milk
¼ teaspoon powdered mace
Salt and pepper
¼ pint cream

METHOD Put the turkey into a large saucepan with carrots, onions, herbs and seasoning, and cover with boiling water. Bring to the boil and skim. Reduce heat and simmer gently for 1¾ hours. Turn off the heat and leave the bird in the water while the sauce is made.

To make the sauce, cut up the white sticks of celery in 1-inch pieces. Boil until tender in the turkey stock. Drain the celery, retaining the liquid. Melt the butter, stir in the flour and cook for 2 minutes. Add the milk and the turkey stock slowly, stirring well, and cook for 10 minutes. Add the cooked celery, mace, salt and pepper. Just before serving, stir in the cream. Lift the turkey on to a serving dish, and pour some of the sauce round it, serving the rest separately.

# Ireland

## COLCANNON

6 helpings

*This vegetable dish is traditionally eaten at Hallowe'en (October 31st), when lucky metal tokens are sometimes concealed in the dish. Correctly the dish should be made with kale, which is improved if cooked in bacon or ham stock.*

METHOD Cook the potatoes and mash them thoroughly. Cook the chopped kale or cabbage, preferably in bacon stock. Chop the onions or leeks and simmer in milk until soft. Add the cooked onions, milk and the butter to the potatoes and beat well, gradually beating in the finely chopped kale. Season generously with pepper and salt. Serve with additional melted butter.

### Ingredients
8 large potatoes
1 pound curly kale or cabbage
6 spring onions or 2 small leeks
⅓ pint creamy milk
1 ounce butter
Salt and pepper

## CHAMP

4 helpings

*This is a very old potato recipe, sometimes called 'Thump'. It is particularly enjoyed by children.*

METHOD Boil the potatoes in salted water. Drain well and dry out by putting a folded cloth over the pan and heating the potatoes gently for a few minutes. Mash the potatoes. Chop the green and white parts of the onions finely and pour boiling water over them. Drain well and add to the milk. Bring milk to the boil and pour on to mashed potatoes. Season to taste with salt and pepper and beat until light and fluffy.

Serve in individual soup-plates in mounds. Scoop out the centre of each mound and pour in melted butter. Each spoonful of potato is dipped in the butter before eating.

### Ingredients
8 large potatoes
10 spring onions
⅓ pint milk
4 tablespoons melted butter
Salt and pepper

## CREAMED CABBAGE

6 helpings

*The Irish are very fond of vegetables in a cream sauce. Cabbage is particularly good cooked this way.*

METHOD Cut the cabbage in quarters and cook in fast-boiling salted water for 5 minutes. Drain very well and cut into narrow strips. Melt the butter in a saucepan and add the cabbage. Stir well and sprinkle in flour, salt and pepper and nutmeg. Stir until the flour is well mixed. Add the milk, put on the lid and cook very gently for 15 minutes.

### Ingredients
1 white cabbage
1 ounce butter
½ ounce plain flour
Salt and pepper
¼ teaspoon ground nutmeg
⅓ pint creamy milk

## SODA BREAD

*This bread can be made brown or white, the brown variety being made with wholewheat flour. Sometimes sultanas are added to the dough, or Treacle Soda Bread can be made by adding black treacle to the white bread mixture.*

METHOD Mix together flour, soda and salt and make a well in the centre. Add milk to make a thick dough and stir with a wooden spoon. The dough should be slack but not wet. Mix the dough lightly and quickly, adding a little extra milk if it seems stiff (brown bread will need additional milk). If a brittle texture is

### Ingredients
1½ pounds plain flour
or
1 pound wholewheat flour and
½ pound plain white flour
1 teaspoon bicarbonate of soda

# Ireland

1 teaspoon salt
½ pint buttermilk or sour milk

GM 6 400°F
200°C

needed, add 1 tablespoon melted butter to the dough. Flatten the dough on a floured board with floured hands, making a circle about 1½-inches thick. Put on to a baking sheet, and mark a large cross with a floured knife. Bake in a fairly hot oven for 40 minutes. To keep the bread soft, wrap in a clean tea towel. Do not cut bread for about 4 hours until it is cold and set. This recipe will make 1 large loaf or 2 small ones.

## BOXTY BREAD

*Boxty is a kind of bread made with potatoes, traditionally eaten at Hallowe'en (October 31st). It can be cooked in the oven, or on a griddle on top of the stove.*

*Ingredients*
1 pound raw potatoes
1 pound cooked mashed potatoes
2 ounces plain flour
1 teaspoon salt
1 teaspoon bicarbonate of soda

GM 4 350°F
180°C

METHOD Grate the raw potatoes and squeeze out the liquid in a clean cloth. Mix with the mashed potatoes. Mix flour, salt and bicarbonate of soda, and add to the potatoes. Roll out on a floured board into a circle ½-inch thick. Cut in 4 quarters and cook on an ungreased griddle for 35 minutes, turning the bread half-way through cooking. It should be well browned on both sides. It can also be cooked in a moderate oven for 35 minutes. Serve hot, split in two with butter. The quarters are called 'farls'.

The same ingredients can be mixed with a little milk to give a dropping consistency and can then be cooked on a lightly greased griddle or thick frying pan as *Boxty Pancakes* to be served with melted butter.

## POTATO CAKES

*Potato cakes are usually served at teatime, very hot with a lot of butter running on them. A few caraway seeds can be added to the mixture. Cold potato cakes are often fried with bacon and eggs for breakfast.*

*Ingredients*
4 ounces plain flour
½ teaspoon baking powder
½ teaspoon salt
1 pound freshly boiled potatoes
2 tablespoons milk

GM 7 425°F
220°C

METHOD Sieve together flour, baking powder and salt and rub in the butter. Mash the potatoes with about 2 tablespoons milk, and add to the flour. Bind the mixture together to make a soft dough. Roll out ¼-inch thick on a well-floured board. Cut in squares or rounds. Cook on an ungreased griddle until brown on both sides, or bake in a hot oven for 20 minutes.

*Soda bread and Whiskey cake.*

# Ireland

## FRUIT BREAD
## BARM BRACK

*This is the only surviving example of the use of yeast in traditional Irish cooking. Barm is the old word for yeast, but the name is derived from* barm breac *– speckled bread. On Hallowe'en it is baked with a gold ring inside, indicating an engagement within a year for the finder. Barm Brack is always sliced and spread with butter before eating.*

METHOD Sieve the flour, nutmeg and salt together. Rub in the butter. Cream the yeast with a little of the sugar. Add remaining sugar to flour mixture. Warm the milk gently, and add to the liquid yeast and eggs (reserve a little egg for glazing the bread). Beat liquid into dry ingredients until batter is stiff but elastic. Fold in the dried fruit and peel, and turn into a buttered 8-inch cake tin. Cover with a cloth and put into a warm place for 1 hour. Brush with beaten egg and bake in a fairly hot oven for 1 hour. Brush over with 1 tablespoon sugar dissolved in 2 tablespoons boiling water, and return to the oven for 3 minutes. Turn out and cool on a wire rack. Serve in slices with butter. When stale, it can be toasted and buttered.

### Ingredients

1 pound plain flour
¼ level teaspoon nutmeg
Pinch of salt
2 ounces butter
¾ ounce fresh yeast
2 ounces sugar
½ pint milk
2 well-beaten eggs
8 ounces sultanas
8 ounces currants
4 ounces mixed chopped candied peel

**GM 6 400°F**
**200°C**

## IRISH WHISKEY CAKE

METHOD Put the whiskey into a small bowl. Peel the orange thinly and soak the rind in the whiskey for a few hours. Discard the peel. Leave the sultanas to soak in the whiskey while preparing the rest of the cake. Cream the butter and sugar. Add the eggs, one at a time, with a teaspoon of flour for each one, beating well between each addition. Sift flour, salt and baking powder together and fold into the egg mixture. Fold in the whiskey and sultanas. Line a greased 7-inch round cake tin with greased paper. Put in the mixture and bake in a moderate oven. Cool on a wire rack. This cake is nicest if eaten while fresh.

### Ingredients

2 tablespoons Irish whiskey
1 orange
6 ounces sultanas
6 ounces butter
6 ounces sugar
3 eggs
8 ounces plain flour
Pinch of salt
1 teaspoon baking powder

**GM 4 350°F**
**180°C**

## DUBLIN CAKE

*This is a typically substantial fruit cake for a family and was formerly made with porter (a type of stout). Today, stout or Guinness can be used. This cake should be sliced and buttered like bread.*

METHOD Cream the butter and the sugar with the lemon rind. Add the eggs one at a time with a teaspoon of flour for each one, beating well between each addition. Sift the remaining flour with soda, salt and spice, and fold into the egg mixture. Moisten with stout or Guinness and stir in the fruit. Line a greased 9-inch round cake tin with greased paper. Put in mixture and bake in a moderate oven for 1½ hours. Reduce heat and continue baking for 1 hour. Cool on a wire rack.

### Ingredients

1 pound plain flour
8 ounces butter
8 ounces brown sugar
Grated rind of 1 lemon
4 eggs
1 teaspoon bicarbonate of soda
½ teaspoon salt
1 teaspoon mixed spice
3 tablespoons stout or Guinness
8 ounces raisins
8 ounces sultanas
8 ounces currants
4 ounces mixed chopped candied peel

**GM 4 350°F reduce to GM 3 325°F**
**180°C                    170°C**

# Italy

The Italians take enormous pleasure in eating their native produce, for this is a rich agricultural country of magnificent fruit and vegetables, hams and sausages, cheeses and wines. Italian food abroad has been debased into dull concoctions of *pasta*, tomatoes, cheese and olives, so the traveller in Italy is unprepared for the variety and delicacy of regional cooking.

Each province or region has its own local specialities which are rarely found in neighbouring areas, so that the dishes of Florence, Venice, Rome, Naples, Bologna and the surrounding country areas for instance, always remain distinctive and original. At the same time dishes depend on seasonal produce, and are never made out of season, so that heavy soups and *pasta* dishes served in winter give way to the raw and stuffed vegetables and piquant cheese are served with the fish dishes of summer.

Lamb, veal and beef are popular meats according to region, cooked with strongly flavoured fresh herbs such as rosemary, basil and origano (a variety of marjoram). Fresh pork appears, but the pig is at its best in beautiful hams and a wide variety of sausages.

Vegetables include peppers, tomatoes, mushrooms, broccoli and fennel, while Italy is abundant in such fruit as figs, apricots, peaches and pears. Potatoes do not appear often in Italian meals, the carbohydrate being provided by the incredible variety of *pasta* made from a flour paste in many shapes completely different from the best-known *macaroni* and *spaghetti*.

Most Italian housewives prefer to shop twice a day, and cook everything freshly for every meal. They like to use lavishly the freshest raw materials, but if there is little time to hand, can concoct a delicious meal from small amounts of simple ingredients. The most basic dish of *pasta* with cheese and butter can be a feast in Italy, although in contrast a cook may spend hours making intricate sauces and stuffings. The appetite is tempted by the vivid colours of both raw materials and finished dishes, with the rich reds of tomatoes and of fish soups, the greens of spinach, herbs, peas and artichokes, and the contrasting creaminess of sauces, pasta and cheeses. The palate is stimulated by the rich smells of Italian cooking, the lavishness and generosity of both the food and the people.

A meal may end with fresh fruit and one of the native cheeses which do not often travel well abroad. Most people only recognise Parmesan, Gorgonzola and Bel Paese, since many Italian cheeses can only be eaten when very fresh and are unlikely to be exported. Ice cream is popular and delectable pastry confections and sweet biscuits, but these are mainly prepared by professional bakers, and there is not the tradition of home-baking found in colder Northern European countries.

# Italy

## VEGETABLE SOUP
## MINESTRONE

*6 helpings*

*Minestrone comes from the great vegetable-growing region of Lombardy and forms a complete meal of vegetables and pasta cooked in broth, flavoured with fresh herbs and cheese.*

### Ingredients

4 ounces dried haricot beans
2 carrots
2 small potatoes
1 small turnip
2 medium onions
1 stick celery
4 tomatoes
½ small cabbage
2 tablespoons olive oil
2 ounces bacon
2 garlic cloves
2 sprigs parsley
3 fluid ounces red wine
3 pints water or stock
2 ounces broken macaroni or spaghetti
2 teaspoons fresh basil
1 tablespoon chopped fresh parsley
Salt and pepper
2 ounces Parmesan cheese

METHOD There are many versions of *Minestrone*. Vegetables such as spinach, small marrows, leeks, peas and beans are often used; sage, marjoram, and thyme can be added; rice is sometimes used instead of pasta.

Soak the dried beans overnight. Slice the carrots, potatoes, turnip, onions and celery, and chop the tomatoes and cabbage. Heat the olive oil and cook the onions until soft and golden. Add the bacon cut in pieces, the garlic and the sprigs of parsley. Add the tomatoes and the red wine, and leave to simmer for 3 minutes. Add drained beans, cover with water or stock, season with salt and pepper and simmer for 2 hours. Add carrots and cook for 15 minutes. Add turnip and potatoes. About 15 minutes before serving time, add celery, cabbage and macaroni or spaghetti. Just before serving, remove the sprigs of parsley, and stir in the chopped parsley and basil. Serve with some grated cheese.

## CHICKEN BROTH WITH POACHED EGGS
## ZUPPA ALLA PAVESE

*4 helpings*

*This is a quickly prepared, nourishing soup which makes a filling meal on its own.*

### Ingredients

1¼ pints chicken stock
4 ½-inch bread slices
2 ounces butter
4 eggs
2 tablespoons grated Parmesan cheese

METHOD Bring the chicken stock to simmering point. Meanwhile, cut the bread in small slices and fry until golden in the butter. Break each egg into a saucer and slide the egg into the hot chicken stock. Gently lift the white over the yolk with a wooden spoon. Cook the eggs for 3 minutes. Gently lift each egg into a soup bowl and pour over the chicken stock. Put grated cheese on each piece of bread, and put bread around eggs. Serve at once.

## BASIL AND GARLIC SAUCE
## PESTO ALLA GENOVESE

*6 helpings*

*This sauce is eaten in Genoa with pasta and gnocchi, and is used as a flavouring for soups; the Genoese basil is supposed to have the best flavour in Italy. Parsley can be used instead of basil, but the flavour is completely different. Walnuts can be used instead of pine nuts.*

### Ingredients

2 ounces fresh basil leaves
2 garlic cloves
Salt
1 ounce pine nuts
2 fluid ounces olive oil

METHOD Pound the basil leaves in a mortar with the garlic, a pinch of salt and the pine nuts, to a thick paste. Gradually add the oil until the mixture is like soft butter. The *Pesto* can be added to cooked drained pasta tossed in butter, or a tablespoonful added to each helping of soup.

74

*Pavese chicken soup.*

# Italy

## HOT ANCHOVY AND GARLIC SAUCE
## LA BAGNA CAUDA

*This sauce comes from Piedmont, and is used with raw
vegetables. It is commonly eaten as a snack with plenty of red
wine.*

### Ingredients
3 fluid ounces olive oil
3 ounces butter
8 anchovy fillets
3 ounces garlic

METHOD Heat the oil and butter and add the anchovies cut in
pieces, and the finely sliced garlic. Simmer for 10 minutes and
keep hot over a spirit lamp. Serve with crisp pieces of raw fennel,
cauliflower or broccoli flowerets, radishes, cabbage or peppers.

## GNOCCHI BAKED WITH BUTTER AND CHEESE
## GNOCCHI ALLA ROMANA

4 helpings

*Gnocchi may be made with semolina, with potatoes, cream
cheese or spinach. This is a simple but delicious dish and it
can be served as a first course. The mixture is easier to handle
if left to set overnight before cutting into shapes.*

### Ingredients
1 pint milk
4 ounces semolina
Salt and pepper
Nutmeg
5 ounces grated Parmesan
cheese
2 eggs
2 ounces butter

GM 6 400°F
200°C

METHOD Bring the milk to the boil, scatter in the semolina and
stir over gentle heat until the mixture is thick enough to support
the spoon. Season well with salt, pepper and ground nutmeg.
Remove pan from the heat and add 3 ounces of the cheese
together with the beaten eggs. When well blended, pour the
mixture into a flat buttered tin about $\frac{1}{4}$-inch deep. Leave until
cold and set.

Cut the mixture into $1\frac{1}{2}$-inch rounds with a pastry cutter, or
into triangles with a knife. Arrange in a buttered fireproof dish,
overlapping the shapes. Dot with butter and remaining cheese,
and bake in a fairly hot oven for 15 minutes. Serve very hot.

## BAKED PASTA LEAVES WITH MEAT SAUCE
## LASAGNE AL FORNO BOLOGNESE

4 helpings

*The rich region of Emilia-Romagne centres round the town of
Bologna, famous for succulent cooking. Lasagne is a type of
macaroni dough made with eggs in long wick flat strips, and
sometimes coloured green with spinach. In this dish, lasagne
is cooked in layers with meat and cream sauces and cheese.*

### Ingredients
8 ounces lasagne
2 ounces butter
1½ ounces plain flour
¾ pint milk
¼ pint double cream
Pinch of ground nutmeg
1 teaspoon salt
3 ounces unsmoked bacon
1 carrot
1 onion
½ stick celery
8 ounces minced lean beef
4 ounces chicken livers
3 teaspoons concentrated
tomato purée
6 fluid ounces white wine

METHOD Boil a large pan of water, throw in the *lasagne*, and
cook for 10-15 minutes until the *lasagne* is tender but still slightly
resistant when bitten. Drain and put into a bowl of cold salted
water.

Melt $1\frac{1}{2}$ ounces butter, and stir in the flour. Pour in the milk
and cream, and stir briskly while cooking until the sauce is
creamy. Remove from heat and season with nutmeg and salt.

Melt the remaining butter and gently brown the bacon cut in
small pieces, together with finely chopped carrot, onion and
celery. Add the minced beef and cook until it has browned
evenly. Add chopped chicken livers and cook for 3 minutes,
then add tomato purée, wine, water or stock, salt and pepper to
taste. Cover the pan and simmer for 45 minutes.

Preheat oven to a moderate level. Butter an ovenproof dish

(about 9 by 12 by 3 inches) and put in a layer of lasagne, then a layer of the meat mixture. Put on a layer of white sauce, then a layer of *lasagne*. Continue in layers, ending with a layer of white sauce. Sprinkle with cheese and bake for 30 minutes.

*½ pint water or stock*
*2 ounces grated Parmesan*
  *cheese*
*Salt and pepper*

**GM 4 350°F**
**180°C**

## EGG NOODLES WITH BUTTER AND CHEESE
## FETTUCCINE AL BURRO

*4 helpings*

*Fettuccine are ¼-inch wide egg noodles, here served plainly with butter and cheese.*

METHOD Drop the *fettuccine* into the boiling water with salt. Stir gently with a wooden fork. Boil rapidly, stirring occasionally for about 8 minutes, until tender but slightly resistant. Drain thoroughly, and toss with plenty of butter and cheese.

*Ingredients*
*1 pound fettuccine*
*8 pints boiling water*
*Salt*
*Unsalted butter*
*Grated Parmesan cheese*

## SPAGHETTI WITH BACON AND EGG
## SPAGHETTI ALLA CARBONARA

*This dish comes from the Abruzzi, where the charcoal burners traditionally stay in the woods for long periods with supplies of spaghetti, ham, oil, hard cheese and eggs.*

METHOD Cook the spaghetti in a large pan of boiling salted water for about 12 minutes until just tender. Drain thoroughly. Meanwhile, cut the bacon into strips and fry in the oil. Serve the spaghetti in deep plates. Break an egg into the centre of each pile of spaghetti, add a portion of bacon and oil, cheese and plenty of pepper. Stir rapidly and serve at once.

*Ingredients*
*1 pound spaghetti*
*8 thick bacon rashers*
*4 tablespoons oil*
*4 eggs*
*4 ounces grated Parmesan*
  *cheese*
*Black pepper*

## VEAL WITH HAM
## SALTIMBOCCA

*4 helpings*

METHOD Cut each escalope into three pieces and flatten them as thin as possible. Cut the ham into similar-sized pieces, and put

# Italy

**Ingredients**
*4 veal escalopes*
*4 slices raw or cooked ham*
*12 sage leaves*
*Salt and pepper*
*Butter*
*6 fluid ounces Marsala (or white wine)*
*Fried bread*

a piece of ham on each piece of veal. Put on a sage leaf and form each piece of veal into a small roll. Tie with cotton, or fix with a small stick. Cook gently in butter until brown all over. Add Marsala or wine and seasoning. Bubble for a minute, then cover the pan and simmer for 15 minutes. Remove cotton or sticks before serving. Garnish with pieces of fried bread.

## VEAL WITH HAM AND CHEESE
## COSTELLETTA ALLA BOLOGNESE

*4 helpings*

**Ingredients**
*4 veal escalopes*
*Beaten egg*
*Breadcrumbs*
*Butter for cooking*
*4 thin slices raw ham*
*4 slices fontina or Gruyère cheese*
*4 tablespoons melted butter*

METHOD The veal escalopes should be beaten thinly and coated with egg and fine breadcrumbs, then fried lightly in butter. When the veal is golden, put a thin slice of ham on top of each escalope (Parma ham is best for this dish). Put 1 slice of cheese on top of each piece of ham, and then the melted butter. Cover the dish and cook for 4 minutes.

## FLORENTINE ROAST PORK
## ARISTA FIORENTINA

*8 helpings*

**Ingredients**
*4 pounds loin of pork*
*3 garlic cloves*
*1 large sprig rosemary*
*3 cloves*
*Salt and pepper*

**GM 4 350°F**
**180°C**

METHOD Take the skin from the meat and trim the fat. Press the garlic into the meat, together with the rosemary and cloves. Rub the joint with salt and pepper and put into a roasting tin. Put 2 inches water into the tin. Roast in a moderate oven for 2½ hours. Leave the meat to cool in its own juice for 20 minutes, and then drain off the liquid. This liquid can be saved, as a layer of good pork fat will settle on the surface. Serve the pork cold.

## LIVER WITH ONIONS
## FEGATO ALLA VENEZIANA

*4 helpings*

*The best calf's liver should be used for this, cut in wafer-thin slices. The liver should be cooked very quickly.*

**Ingredients**
*3 tablespoons olive oil*
*1 pound onions*
*1 pound calf's liver*
*Salt and pepper*

METHOD Heat the oil in a thick shallow pan, and put in very thinly sliced onions. Cook over low heat with a lid on the pan until soft and golden, which will take about 25 minutes. Season with a little salt and black pepper. Put in the liver and cook for 1 minute on each side. Serve at once.

## VEAL WITH MARSALA
## PICCATE AL MARSALA

*4 helpings*

**Ingredients**
*1 pound fillet or leg veal*
*Salt and pepper*
*Lemon juice*
*Flour*
*2 ounces butter*
*4 tablespoons Marsala*
*2 tablespoons beef or chicken stock*

METHOD The veal for this dish should be sliced very thinly, and cut into 3-inch squares. Season each square with salt, pepper and lemon juice, and dust lightly with flour. Melt the butter in a frying pan, put in the pieces of veal and brown quickly on each side. Add the Marsala, and when it bubbles, add the beef or chicken stock. Stir well and simmer for 2 minutes. Serve at once.

## STEWED VEAL
## OSSO BUCCO

*6 helpings*

*This dish should be made from young tender veal, and is usually served with Risotto alla Milanese.*

METHOD The veal should be sawn into pieces 2-inches thick. Brown pieces in the butter and arrange in a heavy shallow fireproof dish with a lid. See that the pieces stand upright, so that the marrow does not fall from the bones. Pour over wine and simmer for 10 minutes. Add stock and skinned and chopped tomatoes. Cover and simmer for 2 hours. The dish may also be cooked in the bottom of a moderate oven.

Mix the grated lemon peel, finely chopped garlic and parsley together and sprinkle on the meat. This is called *gremolata*, and it gives a piquant finish to the dish.

### Ingredients
*4 pounds shin of veal*
*2 ounces butter*
*¼ pint white wine*
*¼ pint stock*
*12 ounces tomatoes*
*Salt and pepper*
*2 teaspoons grated lemon peel*
*1 clove garlic*
*2 tablespoons finely chopped parsley*

# Italy

## TRIPE IN TOMATO SAUCE
## TRIPPA ALLA FIORENTINA

*3 helpings*

*The tripe used in Italy comes from calves and is more delicate than the British ox tripe. Tomato sauce with plenty of herbs and cheese make this delicious and economical dish.*

### Ingredients
*1 pound dressed tripe*
*½ ounce butter*
*1 small onion*
*1 ounce bacon or ham*
*1 pound tomatoes*
*1 garlic clove*
*1 teaspoon basil*
*Salt and pepper*
*Nutmeg*
*1 teaspoon marjoram*
*2 ounces grated Parmesan cheese*

METHOD Boil the tripe for 1 hour, drain and cut into strips 2 inches long and ½-inch wide. Meanwhile prepare the tomato sauce. Melt the butter and fry the chopped onion and bacon until golden. Add peeled chopped tomatoes, crushed garlic, basil, nutmeg, salt and pepper to taste. Cook quickly until the tomatoes are pulped, and put through a sieve. Put the tripe into this sauce, add marjoram and continue to simmer for 1 hour. Serve thickly sprinkled with cheese.

## STUFFED PEPPERS
## PEPERONI RIPIENI

*8 helpings*

*Peppers are used both raw and cooked in a variety of dishes which benefit from their distinctive flavour. Stuffed peppers may be used for a first course, or for a light lunch dish.*

### Ingredients
*4 large green or red peppers*
*4 ounces white bread*
*8 anchovy fillets*
*12 black olives*
*3 sprigs parsley*
*2 garlic cloves*
*½ ounce capers*
*Pepper*
*Marjoram*
*Olive oil*

**GM 3 325°F**
**170°C**

METHOD Cut the peppers in half lengthwise, and remove seeds and membranes. Soak the bread in a little water, and squeeze almost dry. Mix with chopped anchovy fillets, olives and parsley, crushed garlic, capers, and a seasoning of pepper and marjoram. Fill the peppers lightly with this mixture and arrange in a baking dish. Sprinkle generously with olive oil, and cover the dish. Bake in a low oven for 1 hour.

## NEAPOLITAN PIZZA
## PIZZA NAPOLETANA

*4 helpings*

*There are many versions of pizza, but this is the most commonly known recipe. Marjoram may be substituted for origano, and Bel Paese or Gruyère cheese for Mozzarella.*

### Ingredients
*4 ounces plain flour*
*4 fresh tomatoes*
*¼ ounce fresh yeast*
*Salt*
*⅛ pint warm water*
*6 anchovy fillets*
*Origano or basil*
*3 ounces Mozzarella cheese*
*Olive oil*

METHOD Put the flour into a bowl and mix in the salt. Blend the yeast mixed with a little warm water. Mix the flour well with the yeast, and make into a stiff dough with about ⅛th pint of warm water. Knead well until the dough is elastic and light, then cover with a cloth and put in a warm place for about 2 hours until doubled in size. Roll out on a floured board into a large circle about ¼-inch thick. Cover the top of the dough with skinned and coarsely-chopped tomatoes, salt and pepper, thin slices of cheese and anchovy fillets. Sprinkle liberally with origano or basil, and moisten with olive oil. The baking tin should be large enough to allow the pizza to expand during cooking. Bake in a very hot oven for 30 minutes, and serve hot. If Bel Paese cheese is used, it should be added only 10 minutes before the end of cooking time, as it melts quickly. Black olives may be added to the pizza.

**GM 8 450°F
230°C**

*A selection of typical Italian dishes
including (l. to r.): Neopolitan pizza,
minestrone, lasagna a forno bolognese,
stuffed peppers, ham and tomato pizza*

81

# Italy

### FRIED CHEESE SANDWICHES
### MOZZARELLA IN CARROZZA

*4 helpings*

*This popular dish comes from Campania, and is made with Mozzarella – a buffalo cheese. It can be made successfully with Bel Paese.*

**Ingredients**

8 thin slices sandwich bread
8 ounces Mozzarella cheese
2 eggs
Salt
Oil for frying

METHOD Take the crusts from the bread. Put slices of cheese between two slices of bread and cut each 'sandwich' in half. Beat the eggs on a plate with a pinch of salt. Put the sandwiches in the egg and leave for 30 minutes, turning once, so that they are soaked on both sides. Press the edges of the bread together so that the cheese is firmly enclosed. Fry quickly in hot oil, drain on kitchen paper, and serve at once.

### CHICKEN WITH TOMATOES AND MUSHROOMS
### POLLO ALLA CACCIATORA

*4 helpings*

**Ingredients**

1 3-pound roasting chicken
Salt and pepper
Flour
2 ounces butter
1 tablespoon olive oil
2 rashers lean bacon
6 small onions
1 garlic clove
6 fluid ounces dry white wine
2 tomatoes
3 ounces mushrooms
1 tablespoon tomato paste
1 bay leaf
6 tablespoons chicken stock

METHOD Cut the chicken into pieces, season well with salt and pepper, and coat with flour. Melt 1 ounce butter with the oil in a large frying-pan and brown the chicken. Cut the bacon into small pieces, and brown in the remaining butter with the onions and crushed garlic. Add the chicken pieces and wine, and cook quickly to reduce wine. Add peeled and crushed tomatoes, sliced mushrooms, tomato paste, bayleaf and stock. Bring to the boil, then simmer until tender for about 30 minutes.

### PEPPERS WITH TOMATOES AND ONIONS
### PEPERONATA

*6 helpings*

*This can be served hot before or with the main course. It can be reheated, and is also very good served cold.*

**Ingredients**

8 red peppers
10 large ripe tomatoes
1 large onion
1 ounce butter
2 tablespoons olive oil
Salt

METHOD Remove the seeds from the peppers, and slice the flesh into strips. Peel the tomatoes and cut in quarters. Slice the onion very thinly. Heat the butter and oil and brown the onion lightly. Add the peppers, season with salt, cover and simmer for 15 minutes. Add the tomatoes and continue cooking for 30 minutes, uncovered, and stirring lightly, until the mixture is almost dry.

### MILANESE RICE
### RISOTTO ALLA MILANESE

*6 helpings*

*There are a number of variations of this dish, but saffron appears in all of them. Risotto can be served as an accompaniment to a dish (see Osso Bucco) or on its own with butter and cheese, or with the addition of pieces of poultry, game, shellfish, poultry livers or vegetables.*

METHOD Wash and dry the rice well. Melt half the butter and fry

# Italy

the finely chopped onion until golden. Add the beef marrow, which gives a rich flavour, but is not essential. Add the rice and cook for a few minutes, stirring well until it is soaked in the butter. Add boiling stock and cook for 10 minutes. Add the wine. Pound 3 or 4 filaments of saffron to a powder and soak the powder in a few spoonfuls of the stock for about 5 minutes. Strain the liquid into the rice. Cook for 10 minutes until the liquid is absorbed. Take off heat, stir in remaining butter and cheese, season well, and leave to stand for 5 minutes before serving.

**Ingredients**
*12 ounces Italian rice
   (or long-grain rice)*
*4 ounces butter*
*1 small onion*
*2 ounces chopped beef marrow
   (optional)*
*3 pints stock*
*6 fluid ounces dry white wine*
*Saffron*
*Salt and pepper*
*3 ounces grated Parmesan
   cheese*

*Baked artichokes, here served whole.*

## SWEET AND SOUR ONIONS
## CIPOLLINE IN AGRODOLCE

*These onions may be served hot or cold. The recipe is best made with small pickling onions.*

METHOD Put the unpeeled onions into boiling water, and cook for 10 minutes. Peel them, and put into a pan with olive oil, cloves, bay leaf and salt. Simmer for 5 minutes. Add the vinegar and sugar, and cook until the sauce is syrupy.

### Ingredients
*1 pound small onions*
*2 tablespoons olive oil*
*2 cloves*
*1 bay leaf*
*Salt*
*2 tablespoons vinegar*
*1 tablespoon sugar*

## MIXED FRIED VEGETABLES
## FRITTO MISTO DI VERDURE

*4 helpings*

*All kinds of food can be cut into small pieces and fried in a crisp batter. A mixture of fish is popular, and also a mixture of chicken, sweetbreads, brains and vegetables. This simple dish makes an excellent light meal.*

METHOD Peel the aubergines, and cut them in lengthwise slices. Cover with water to which a few drops of lemon juice have been added, and leave to drain for 1 hour. Do not peel the courgettes, but cut them in long slices and cover with salt, leave to drain for 1 hour. Cut the cheese in slices $\frac{1}{8}$ inch thick (Bel Paese may be used).

Put the flour, warm water, oil and salt into a bowl, and stir to a smooth cream. Beat the egg white stiffly, and fold into the batter just before using. Dip ingredients into batter and fry in very hot oil. Drain on kitchen paper and serve quickly.

### Ingredients
*1 pound aubergines*
*1 pound courgettes*
*8 ounces Mozzarella cheese*
*4 ounces plain flour*
*¼ pint warm water*
*2½ tablespoons oil*
*½ teaspoon salt*
*1 egg white*

## BAKED STUFFED ARTICHOKES
## CARCIOFI AL TEGAME ALLA ROMANA

*4 helpings*

METHOD Trim the bases of the artichokes so that they stand flat. Rub any cut surfaces with lemon juice to prevent discoloration. Trim off bruised and loose leaves, and slice 1 inch from the top of the artichoke. Trim the points from each leaf with scissors. Cook artichokes for 10 minutes in a large pan of boiling water. Drain and cool upside down in a sieve. Spread apart the top leaves and pull out the fluffy 'choke' to leave the heart clean. Drop a little lemon juice into each artichoke.

Heat the oil in a pan, and add breadcrumbs. Cook over a moderate heat, stirring well for 2 minutes, until crisp and lightly coloured. Remove from heat and stir in crushed garlic, vinegar, finely chopped mint, salt and pepper. Divide the stuffing between the artichokes. Put about 2 tablespoons stuffing in the centre of each, and press remaining stuffing between outer leaves. Put artichokes close together in a deep baking dish and pour in 1 inch boiling water. Cover the dish tightly and bake in a moderate oven for 1 hour. They may be served hot, or brushed with olive oil and served cold with lemon quarters.

### Ingredients
*4 small artichokes*
*Lemon juice*
*5 tablespoons olive oil*
*3 ounces fresh white breadcrumbs*
*2 garlic cloves*
*1 tablespoon wine vinegar*
*2 teaspoons chopped fresh mint*
*Salt and pepper*

**GM 4 350°F**
**180°C**

85

# Italy

### RICE AND PEAS
### RISI E BISI

*6 helpings*

*This is a favourite Venetian dish, a little more liquid than Risotto.*

*Ingredients*
*2 pints chicken stock*
*3 ounces butter*
*1 small onion*
*4 ounces cooked smoked ham (optional)*
*2 pounds unshelled peas (12 ounces peas when shelled)*
*12 ounces Italian rice (long-grain rice can be substituted)*
*2 ounces grated Parmesan cheese*

METHOD Simmer the chicken stock. Melt 2 ounces butter over moderate heat and cook chopped onion until transparent but not brown. Add diced ham, shelled peas and rice. Stir well until the butter has been absorbed. Pour in half the stock, and cook uncovered for 5 minutes, stirring occasionally. Add more stock, without stirring, and continue adding stock until it has all been used. Do not stir too much or the peas will break. Stir in the remaining butter and the cheese, and serve while hot and creamy.

### LEMON WATER ICE
### GRANITA DI LIMONE

*6 helpings*

*Italy has a great reputation for delicious ices. The water-ices are particularly refreshing at the end of a meal, and may be made in the ice-making compartment of a refrigerator.*

*Ingredients*
*1 pint water*
*4 ounces sugar*
*½ pint lemon juice*

METHOD Bring the water and sugar to the boil, and boil for 5 minutes. Cool and mix with the lemon juice. Freeze in the ice compartment of a refrigerator at the normal temperature for making ice. Stir two or three times, and allow three hours to freeze.

*A typical selection of Italian desserts is both attractive and delicious.*

## WHIPPED EGG WITH MARSALA
## ZABAIONE

*4 helpings*

METHOD Put the yolks, egg and sugar into the top of a double saucepan over simmering water. Beat with a balloon whisk or rotary beater until pale yellow and fluffy. Gradually add Marsala and continue beating until thick enough to hold the shape of a spoon. This will take about 10 minutes. Spoon into warm glasses and serve at once.

*Ingredients*
*5 egg yolks*
*1 egg*
*2 ounces castor sugar*
*¼ pint Marsala*

## CARAMEL ORANGES
## ARANCI CARAMELLIZZATI

*4 helpings*

*This recipe should be prepared with seedless oranges but any variety is good treated this way.*

METHOD Peel the oranges very carefully with a very sharp knife, so that no pith is left on them, Dissolve sugar in water and boil until it is thick. Dip the oranges in for about 2 minutes, turning so that they are coated in syrup. Arrange in a large serving dish. Take all pith from the peel and then cut peel as thinly as possible into slices as long as matchsticks. Put into boiling water and cook for 7 minutes until the peel loses its bitterness. Drain, and then cook in the syrup until transparent and becoming caramelised, but do not let the mixture turn into toffee. Put a spoonful of the peel on top of each orange, pour the remaining syrup on, and serve very cold.

*Ingredients*
*4 oranges*
*6 ounces sugar*
*¼ pint water*

# Luxemburg

This ancient Grand Duchy is roughly equal in size to the county of Warwickshire in England, or Rhode Island in the United States. The population of under 350,000 is fortunate in occupying a country of such immense variety. Wedged between French Lorraine and the German Rhineland with Belgium to the North, Luxemburg has managed to maintain a strong individuality throughout its long history. Although French and German are the official languages, the Luxemburg tongue (Luxemburgeois) is still used in everyday conversation. Similarly, their cooking has kept its own personality.

Over a third of the Grand Duchy is covered by woodland providing fine game in the autumn shooting season. The hills and mountainsides of the northern Luxemburg Ardennes region also rear pigs for the delicate ham which makes an ideal first course at dinner. Luxemburgers themselves usually eat it during the day in large rye bread sandwiches.

The south of the country has richly cultivated rolling farmlands. Apples, blackcurrants and quetsch plums grow in the orchards and fields. These are used in the making of fruit liqueurs. The hops are sent to breweries in the north and south of the country. The grape-growing valley of the Moselle runs along the border with Western Germany in the south eastern corner of Luxemburg. The delicate golden grapes are made into Moselle white wine which is drunk throughout the year. Wines reserved for the more special occasions include Riesling, Anxerois, Pinot, Rulander and Traminer. Fresh grape juice is also popular.

The rivers and the Upper Sûre lake provide an abundance of fish for the freshwater angler. Among the most popular are the bream, pike, gudgeon, trout and rainbow trout.

As well as featuring the famous processions, the carnivals and wine festivals are the occasion for the preparation of sugared fried pastries cut in strips and knotted, called *Les Pensées Bromillées* in French and *Verwenrlter Gedanken* in Luxemburgeois. Pastries are also often eaten through the year with favourites adapted from Luxemburg's neighbours. The unsalted curd cheesecake known as *Kaes Kuch* is a national speciality.

# Luxemburg

## HARE IN CREAM SAUCE
## HUES ENCIVI

*3-4 helpings*

*This classic dish is a well-known national one, widely eaten during the shooting season, especially in September. The meat, cream and caper seasoning provide exciting contrasts in flavour, yet blend into a luxurious whole.*

### Ingredients

*1 saddle of hare*
*Larding bacon*
*Salt and freshly ground*
*black pepper*
*3-4 rashers fat bacon*
*2-3 sprigs parsley*
*1 carrot*
*1 onion*
*½ bay leaf*
*Good pinch grated nutmeg*
*¼-½ pint white stock*
*3 tablespoons flour*
*1 pint white stock or water*
*½ pint double cream*
*Capers*
*1 teaspoon dry mustard*
*1 tablespoon white wine*
*vinegar*
*Slices of lemon*
*Boiled, buttered noodles*

METHOD Clean the saddle and trim it. Lard with strips of fat bacon, and season well with the salt and pepper. Cut the rind off the rashers and put into a stewpan. Add the parsley, a scraped and chopped carrot, a peeled and chopped onion, bay leaf and nutmeg. Put in a teacupful (about $\frac{5}{8}$ pint) of stock, with the saddle, spine uppermost. Cover the pan, bring the stock gently to the boil, and let the dish simmer over low heat until the meat is tender. (The time will depend on the age and size of the hare, and how it was shot). Add more stock if the dish shows any signs of drying out. Remove the hare when ready. Cover, and keep warm while you prepare the sauces.

Cream the flour with a little cold stock. Stir the creamed mixture into the liquid in the pan, which should be well reduced. Simmer together until the flour is blended in and lightly browned. Add the 1 pint of white stock or water, and bring to the boil. Stir as it heats. When it boils, remove the pan from the heat, and strain the liquid into a second pan. Gradually trickle in the cream continuously.

Reheat the sauce, still stirring, until it is near (but not at) boiling point. Add drained, chopped capers, a little at a time, until the flavour is strong enough. Stir in the mustard and vinegar. Replace the hare in the sauce, and keep over heat but under boiling point for about 15 minutes. Serve the hare on a heated platter, and coat well with the sauce. Garnish with capers, and the lemon slices. Serve with the noodles as an ideal complement to the hare's flavours.

## APPLE CAKE
## APPEL KUCH

*First-quality fruit and pastries are the pride of the Grand Duchy's farmers and their wives, and both products have achieved an international reputation.*

METHOD Sift the flour and baking powder together. Mix all the dry ingredients. Rub in the butter lightly. Then mix to a springy dough with the milk.

Roll out or pat into shape. Grease a loaf pan about 9 by 5 by 3 inches, and lay the dough in it. Alternatively, use a 7-inch round sandwich tin.

METHOD Peel and core the apples. Slice them in thin segments, and lay them in overlapping lines or circles on the dough. Cover with a custard made by heating the milk with the 3 ounces sugar and the cinnamon, pouring on the eggs and reheating gently until thick. Pour this custard over the apples. Bake the cake for about 30 minutes in a fairly hot oven at the temperature below until the dough is cooked through. Serve hot or cold, with plenty of cream.

### Ingredients
**Dough**
*8 ounces flour*
*2 teaspoons baking powder*
*1 tablespoon sugar*
*½ teaspoon salt*
*4 ounces butter*
*¼ pint plus 4 tablespoons milk*

**Topping**
*Sharp eating apples*
*2 eggs, well beaten*
*⅝ pint milk*
*½ teaspoon ground cinnamon*
*3 ounces castor sugar*

**GM 5 375°F**
**190°C**

## LUXEMBURG'S OWN CHEESECAKE
## KAES KUCH

*Although cheesecakes are made the world over, Luxemburg's is an unusual combination of low-fat cheese and a rich dough. Make the same dough as for the Apple Pudding or Cake, and put it in the same pan.*

METHOD For the cheese mixture make sure the cheese is free from lumps. Beat the egg yolks until liquid. Mix them with the cheese, and stir well, to blend them in. Lastly, sift in 3 ounces sugar with the salt. Mix thoroughly. Pour this mixture on to the dough. Bake in a fairly hot oven at the first temperature for about 35 minutes or until the dough is firm and cooked through.

Shortly before the end of the cooking time, whip the egg whites until stiff. Sift in half the remaining sugar gradually, while whipping. Continue whipping until the meringue is really stiff and glossy. Fold in the last of the sugar. Reduce the oven heat to cool. Take out the hot cheesecake and pile the meringue on top, taking care to seal the edge over the cheesecake mixture. Replace in the oven until the meringue is set and slightly brown.

### Ingredients

**Cheese Mixture:**
*1 pound unsalted curd cheese*
  *or home-made, soft cheese*
*3 eggs, separated*
*Scant ¼ pint double cream*
*Juice and grated rind of ½*
  *lemon*
*4 ounces castor sugar*
*¼ teaspoon salt*

**GM 5 375°F**
**190°C**
**reducing to**
**GM 2 300°F**
**150°C**

# Netherlands

Dutch cooking has a definite character, and an unusual one for a northern people. It has been shaped by her history, dating from the medieval days when merchant sailing ships first brought spices from the distant East to the quays of old Amsterdam, for sale to all Europe. The seafaring ships soon ranged farther afield; to the spices of Indonesia and the fruits of Africa were added the products of Central America, notably coffee and chocolate and strange fruits. Colonisation followed; Holland gained possessions from South Africa to New York (originally called New Amsterdam), from Indonesia to the West Indies. The ways of life in these places influenced the Dutch people's customs deeply, and have done so ever since.

They do so still, and notably in cookery. Rice features much in their meals, for instance, and the old fragrant spices still pervade the kitchens. Cinnamon and nutmeg are used lavishly, and so are hot pickles and sauces. Worcester Sauce, which is often thought to be typically English, is one of them. Dutch coffee and chocolate, too, have their own redolence, and are well known and loved wherever they are used.

Those old merchant spice importers succeeded because they believed in solid worth. Their pictures, their homes, their fabrics, all bore witness to it. So did their food; and today Dutch cooking displays the same virtue. The fish in the coastal waters is plentiful and cheap, and the Dutch use it well and to their profit. Their smoked eel, for instance, is a renowned delicacy throughout Europe, and many of her fresh eel dishes deserve to be better known beyond her borders. So, too, do her people's ways with the abundant herrings.

On land, the low-lying drained pastures feed cattle which give the Dutch rich dairy goods. As a nation, they enjoy them to the full, especially butter, and varied mild, creamy cheeses. They combine these dairy products with grain in delicious 'baked goods', often richly spiced. Their butter cakes, cookies and traditional biscuits are ideal for nibbling with the fragrant coffee and chocolate, and the liqueurs which are their pride too.

The Dutch eat amply, and they certainly eat well.

# Netherlands

## PICKLED HERRING SALAD
## HARINGSLA

*Northern Europe's seafaring peoples have gathered the harvest of the sea since time immemorial. Herrings have always been among their staple foods.*

*The Dutch have their own characteristic ways of preparing them. This is one of the most popular, a favourite everywhere in Holland; it has a fresh, sweet-sharp flavour.*

### Ingredients

1 lettuce (inner leaves only)
3 apples
3 pickled herring, chopped
3 hard-boiled eggs, chopped
2 boiled beetroot, peeled and cubed in ½-inch dice
8 cold boiled potatoes, mashed
3 large sweet pickled gherkins, sliced
½ medium-sized onion, peeled and finely chopped
French dressing
Mayonnaise
Garnish:
2 hard-boiled eggs
Sliced pickled gherkins
1 tablespoon chopped parsley

METHOD Decorate an oblong dish with the lettuce leaves. Peel core and dice the apples. Mix immediately with the herring, add all the other ingredients except the Mayonnaise and garnish, and toss them together in the dressing. Spread the mixture evenly over the lettuce leaves, and cover generously with mayonnaise. Decorate with the garnish.

For the garnish, chop the egg whites. Rub the yolks through a sieve. Scatter both on the mayonnaise with the slices of gherkin and the parsley.

## EEL SOUP
## PALING SOEP

4-6 helpings

*Eel, fresh or smoked, is popular throughout Holland, and is prepared in many different ways. Smoked eel is a delicacy known internationally, but this Eel Soup, excellent as it is, is seldom seen outside the country.*

### Ingredients

1 tablespoon salt
6-8 peppercorns
½ bay leaf
1½ pounds eel, cleaned and cut in 1-inch pieces
6 tablespoons butter
3 tablespoons flour
1 tablespoon parsley, chopped
2 egg yolks

METHOD Bring 2 pints water to the boil, with the salt, peppercorns and bay leaf. Add the eel, and simmer gently for 20 minutes. Remove the eel.

Melt the butter in a saucepan, add the flour, and cook them together for 2-3 minutes. Trickle in the eel stock, stirring briskly. Simmer for 15 minutes, then sieve. Add the eel and parsley to the thickened soup. Reheat gently. Remove from the heat when really hot. Beat the egg yolks with a little of the hot soup. Pour the mixture into the soup, stir well, and serve.

## VERMICELLI SOUP WITH MEAT BALLS
## VERMICELLI SOEP MET BALLETJES

6 helpings

*Little savoury meat balls are always served in this, as with many other Dutch soups and stews.*

### Ingredients

1 quart bone stock (or stock from a bouillon cube)
2 blades mace
2 ounces fine vermicelli

METHOD Add the mace to the stock, and simmer for 15 minutes. Crush the vermicelli lightly. Make the meat balls. Mix all the ingredients well, and roll into small balls. Bring the soup to the boil, add the meat balls and vermicelli, cover the pan and boil gently for 10 minutes. Remove the mace, pour into a tureen or soup plates. Garnish with the parsley, and serve at once.

94

*Vermicelli soup cooking
with small meat balls.*

Meat balls:
*2 slices white bread without
    crusts, soaked in a very little
    milk*
*½ pound minced steak or veal*
*1 egg*
*½ teaspoon salt*
*¼ teaspoon nutmeg, grated*
*Chopped parsley*

# Netherlands

### CARP WITH RAISIN SAUCE
### KARPER MET ROZIJNEN SAUS

*4-5 helpings*

*The sweet-sour sauce, here served with carp, is equally good with other freshwater fish, which can sometimes have a muddy taste.*

*Ingredients*

*1 carp*
*½ ounce salt per pint of water*
*½ pint white wine*
*5 tablespoons sugar*
*. Juice of 1 lemon*
*1 teaspoon grated lemon rind*
*2 tablespoons butter*
*4 ounces seedless raisins*

METHOD Tie the carp in muslin after cleaning it, and simmer in at least 2 pints water for 30-40 minutes or until tender but still firm. Leave the fish in the liquid.

Take ½ pint of this fish stock, and add wine, sugar, lemon juice and rind, butter and raisins. Simmer very gently, to make a smooth sauce. Taste, and reseason if you wish. Bring the carp to the boil in the remaining liquid, to reheat it. Remove it to a warmed serving dish, and pour the hot sauce over.

### FRIED SALT HERRINGS WITH RED CABBAGE
### GEBAKKEN BOKKING

*This is perhaps the most 'national' of all the Dutch recipes for preparing herrings. The red cabbage makes an ideal companion to the juicy, crisped fish.*

*Ingredients*

*1 salt herring or bloater per person*
*Salt and pepper if required*
*Flour*
*Clarified butter*
*Red cabbage*

METHOD Take the heads off the herrings. Open the fish, and remove the bones. Flatten the split fish, and season them if they need it. Sprinkle with flour, and shake off the excess. Heat the clarified butter in a frying pan, and fry the fish gently on both sides until cooked through. Have a well-heated flat dish ready, and the cooked, hot red cabbage, well-drained. Make a bed of the cabbage, and lay the fried fish on it ready to serve.

Another popular Dutch vegetable to serve with these fried herrings is a purée of potatoes and apples.

### MOCK FINCHES
### BLINDE VINKEN

*4 helpings*

*This simple but savoury dish of veal fillets stuffed with bacon is tastier and easier to eat than any real small birds would be.*

*Ingredients*

*4 veal escalopes, 4-5 ounces each*
*4 ounces streaky, smoked bacon, minced*
*1 egg*
*2 tablespoons soft white breadcrumbs*
*1 teaspoon chopped parsley*
*Pepper, salt and nutmeg to taste*
*1 ounce unsalted butter*
*⅛ pint stock (veal or chicken)*
*Slices of fresh lemon*

METHOD Trim the veal of any ragged edges, and beat flat if at all thick. Mix together the bacon, breadcrumbs, parsley and seasoning to suit your taste. Beat the egg, and bind the mixture with it. Divide the mixture into 4 portions, and spread 1 portion over each slice of veal. Roll up and secure with cotton. Heat the butter in a shallow flame-proof casserole and fry the rolls on all sides lightly. Add the stock, and cover with lemon slices. Place a lid on the pan, and simmer very gently for 30 minutes. Remove the thread, and serve very hot.

# Netherlands

## VEAL WITH CREAM SAUCE
## KALFSOESTER MET ROOMSAUS

*4 helpings*

*Dutch housewives combine their dairy products with many spicy flavourings, but none is better than this smooth sauce over a white meat.*

METHOD Beat the escalopes to flatten them if necessary. Heat the butter in a frying pan, and fry the escalopes lightly on both sides. Remove from the heat. Pour the remaining butter into an oven-proof dish, and swirl it to coat the dish evenly. Place the escalopes in the dish, in one layer. Put a slice of cheese and a bacon rasher on each piece of meat. Bake, uncovered, in a fairly hot oven for 15 minutes. While the meat bakes, blend the cream with the tomato purée and sugar. Pour this mixture round the veal, and bake the dish for another 5 minutes. Garnish with sprigs of parsley before serving.

**Ingredients**
*4 veal escalopes*
*2 ounces unsalted butter*
*4 wafer-thin slices Gouda cheese*
*4 thin rashers bacon without rind*
*Salt and pepper*
*¼ pint double cream*
*1 tablespoon tomato purée*
*½ teaspoon granulated sugar*
*Parsley to garnish*
**GM 6 400°F**
**200°C**

## HUNTERS' STEW
## JACHTSCHOTEL

*4 helpings*

*Although this dish may be derived from neighbouring Germany, it bears strong marks of Dutch influence. It is extremely popular everywhere in Holland.*

METHOD Fry the onions in 1½ ounces butter until soft and pale golden-brown. Trim the meat, and strain the stock if necessary. Use the extra ½ ounce butter to grease an ovenproof dish. Place alternate layers of meat, potatoes and peeled slices of the apples in the dish, ending with a layer of potatoes. Sprinkle all over with the breadcrumbs. Melt the extra ounce of butter, and trickle it all over the crumbs. Bake the dish in a fairly hot oven for 20 minutes.

**Ingredients**
*½ pound onions, peeled and sliced*
*2 ounces unsalted butter*
*½-¾ pound cooked meat, finely chopped*
*½ pint stock*
*1 pound cold boiled potatoes, mashed*
*½ pound sour cooking apples*
*Salt, pepper and nutmeg*
*1 tablespoon breadcrumbs*
*1 ounce extra butter*
**GM 5 375°F**
**190°C**

## STEWED STEAK WITH ONIONS
## HACHEE

*8 helpings*

*This savoury beef and onion stew is popular with Dutch housewives because they can use leftover meat and vegetables. Hachee can be served either with mashed potatoes and cabbage or with root vegetables.*

METHOD Cut any gristle or ragged ends off the meat. Heat the butter and oil in a heavy flameproof casserole, and fry the meat on all sides until it is beginning to brown. (Cooked meat will take about 5 minutes, raw meat 7-10 minutes.) Add the onions and fry gently for 5 minutes, stirring. Stir in the flour. Then pour in the stock, already warmed, and stir to blend.

Bring the mixture to the boil. Add the bay leaves, peppercorns and seasoning. Leave to simmer for 1 hour, covered with a lid. Taste, and adjust the seasoning if required. Serve in the casserole.

**Ingredients**
*1½ pounds stewing steak or cooked cold meat, cut in cubes*
*1 ounce dripping*
*1 tablespoon cooking oil*
*1 pound onions, peeled and sliced*
*1 ounce flour*
*1 pint brown stock*
*2 bay leaves*
*4 peppercorns*
*Salt and pepper*
*1 tablespoon vinegar*
*1 tablespoon Worcester Sauce*

97

# Netherlands

## SAUERKRAUT WITH BACON
## ZUURKOOL MET SPEK

*6 helpings*

*Sauerkraut is a national favourite among vegetables, and this dish with bacon is one of the best-known and liked of all the ways of serving it.*

### Ingredients

2½ pounds sauerkraut
Scant ½ pint water
3 tablespoons butter
Salt
1-1½ pounds hot boiled bacon
or
1-1½ pounds gammon joint

METHOD Place the sauerkraut in boiling, salted water. Simmer for 20-30 minutes. Check during the last few minutes that the saucepan is not completely dry, as the liquid should wholly evaporate save for a few drops. Melt the butter, and add it to the hot sauerkraut in the saucepan. Stir for a few moments to mix in well. Slice the bacon or gammon. Lay the sauerkraut in a shallow, warmed serving dish with the bacon or gammon slices on top. Serve as soon as possible, while the meat is still fresh and moist. Potatoes or green bean purée are sometimes served with this spicy dish and sausages are a good alternative to ham.

## PORK AND RICE DISH
## NASI GORENG

*6 helpings*

*Indonesian cookery is popular throughout the Netherlands. Rijsttafel (Rice Table) is a tremendous spread of countless varieties of rice and spicy dishes made with fish, meat and vegetables, all with an exotic flavour and aroma.*

*Nasi Goreng is also an Indonesian dish. It consists of fried rice with pork and spices, topped with thin strips of omelet and served with numerous side dishes. It can be made at home or bought ready-made from one of the many Indonesian restaurants.*

METHOD Cook the rice in boiling salted water for about 12 minutes. Turn into a sieve, and separate the rice grains by rinsing with cold running water until the surplus starch is removed. Allow to drain. Cut the onions in rings, and fry in half the butter (2 ounces) in a large pan, together with the pork cut into cubes. Brown slowly for about 20 minutes over medium heat. Add the remaining butter, rice, mixed vegetables, pepper, salt, curry powder and soy sauce. Blend well over the medium heat until piping hot. Turn into an ovenproof dish, and garnish with strips of omelet. Arrange small wedges of tomato round the edge of the dish. Flash under a hot grill for a moment or two. Then serve immediately, with peanuts, shrimp crisps and a green salad.

### Ingredients

½ pound Patna rice
4 ounces butter
12 ounces shoulder of pork
12 ounces mixed cooked
  vegetables
½ pound onions
2 tablespoons soy sauce
1 level teaspoon curry powder
Pepper and salt
2 tomatoes
1 thin one-egg omelet, fried
  flat like a pancake and
  turned

# Netherlands

### CURLY KALE WITH SMOKED SAUSAGES
### BOERENKOOL MET ROOKWORST

*4-6 helpings*

*Ingredients*
*2 pounds kale*
*2 pounds potatoes*
*2 ounces crushed or porridge oats*
*6 large smoked sausages*
*6 ounces streaky bacon*
*Salt, pepper and nutmeg*

METHOD Clean the kale, and strip off the stalk and vein together. Chop roughly. Peel and cube the potatoes. Cook the kale and bacon together in a little boiling water, salted if necessary, for 10 minutes. Add the cubed potatoes and the oats. Prick the sausages, and place them on top of the mixture. Cover the pan with a lid, and boil gently until the kale is tender and the potatoes are soft; this takes about 30 minutes. Remove the sausages and bacon, and mash the potatoes and kale together. Season as required. Replace the sausages and bacon, and serve with plenty of mustard.

### BROWN BEANS AND BACON
### BRUINE BONEN

*4 helpings*

**This makes a substantial supper dish.**

*Ingredients*
*2 pounds dried brown beans*
*1 teaspoon salt*
*1 pound streaky smoked bacon without rinds*
*6 onions, peeled and sliced in rings*

METHOD Soak the beans in water overnight. Next day, bring to the boil in the same water, and cook gently for about 1 hour. Add the salt after 30 minutes. Drain the beans once cooked, and keep them warm. Dice the bacon small. Fry gently until crisp. Remove from the pan, and mix with the beans. Fry the onion rings in the same fat. Scatter them over the beans, or serve separately if you prefer. Also serve sweet pickled gherkins and strong mustard.

### RED CABBAGE
### RODE KOOL

*4 helpings*

**Red cabbage is popular because it keeps well, and can be reheated without harm. This sweet-sour way of cooking is widely used; where the vegetable is served with many meat dishes.**

*Ingredients*
*1 pound red cabbage*
*¼ pint water*
*4 cloves*
*1 pound sour cooking apples*
*2 ounces sugar*
*2 ounces butter*
*2 tablespoons mild vinegar*
*1 teaspoon salt*

METHOD Trim, clean and shred the cabbage. Peel, core and slice the apples. Place in a pan with the water, and the cloves, sugar and salt. Cover with a lid, bring to near boiling point, and simmer gently until tender. It will take about 1 hour. Remove the cloves. Add the butter and vinegar. Blend well over the heat. Taste, reseason if necessary, and serve hot with any strongly flavoured meat dish.

### BEETS WITH APPLES
### BIETEN MET APPELEN

*4-6 helpings*

*Ingredients*
*2 large cooked beets*
*5 tablespoons salted butter*
*4 sour cooking apples, peeled and finely chopped*
*1 onion, peeled and shredded*
*Salt*
*Nutmeg, grated*

METHOD Peel and slice the beets. Place them in a saucepan with the butter, apples, onion, salt and a generous amount of grated nutmeg. Mix well. Place over gentle heat, and simmer until both vegetable and fruit are reduced to a purée. Beets with apples can be served with almost any hot main course dish.

## BOILED RICE
## RIJS

*This way of cooking rice is used for both savoury and sweet dishes. It is popular as a sweet dish, for instance, with the cinnamon sauce served with groats.*

METHOD Wash the rice under cold running water until the water runs clear. Place in a saucepan with twice its volume of cold water. Bring to the boil quickly, with the saucepan covered. Simmer for 10 minutes. Remove the lid, and allow the rice to stand for 10 minutes until all the liquid has evaporated. Toss lightly with a fork, and use as you wish.

## GROATS WITH CINNAMON SAUCE
## GORT MET KANEELSAUS

*Groats, known in Britain as hulled wheat or oats, or as crushed or rolled grains, are used a great deal in Holland, both for porridge and for various sweet dishes. This is one of the classic ways of serving them.*

METHOD Wash the grain. Soak in cold water until soft. Boil in the same water, very gently, for about 2 hours, until porridgy.

To make the sauce, moisten the mixed flour and sugar with a little of the milk. Place the rest of the milk in a saucepan with the cinnamon stick, and bring gently to the boil. Either simmer until the milk is well flavoured, or allow the cinnamon stick to infuse in the milk until the same result is obtained. Stir a little more milk into the flour and sugar mixture, and mix well. Continue adding milk gradually until the mixture is liquid. Tip the mixture into the remaining milk, stir, and heat until at simmering point. Simmer for 5 minutes, remove the cinnamon stick, and use.

*Ingredients*
Groats
*Hulled wheat, or rolled oats*
*Water*
Sauce
*½ pint milk*
*2 ounces flour*
*4 tablespoons granulated sugar*
*1 stick cinnamon*

## THIN FILLED PANCAKES
## FLENJES

*These pancakes are often eaten just with brown sugar or maple syrup.*

# Netherlands

## Ingredients

**Batter**
4 ounces plain flour
Pinch of salt
1 egg
½ pint milk
**Optional Filling**
Strawberry jam
¼ pint whipped cream

METHOD Sieve the flour and salt into a basin, and make a well in the centre. Beat the egg slightly and mix with the milk. Pour the egg-milk mixture into the flour gradually, and beat to make a smooth batter. Grease a 5-inch frying pan with a little butter. Heat the pan until the fat shows a faint blue haze. Pour in enough batter to cover the bottom of the pan. Allow the pancake to brown on the underside; turn over with a spatula and brown the second side slightly. Remove to greaseproof paper. Make the rest of the pancakes in the same way.

When the pancakes are cold you can spread all except one with strawberry jam and whipped cream. Keep enough whipped cream to decorate the top one. Pile the pancakes one on top of another to form a 'layer cake' with the plain pancake on top. Sprinkle with grated chocolate, and decorate with halved glacé cherries and whipped cream.

## CHERRY FLAN
## LIMBURGSE VLAAI

*8 helpings*

*Limburg, in the south-east corner of the Netherlands, is famous for two reasons. First, it is the only part of the Netherlands which can be called hilly, although it is less than 1,000 feet high. Second, the region is the home of this delicious* Limburgse vlaai.

## Ingredients

**Pastry**
6 ounces plain flour
4 ounces unsalted butter
2 ounces castor sugar
1 egg yolk

**Filling**
1 x 14- or 15-ounce can Morello cherries in syrup
¼ pint cherry juice from the can
1 heaped tablespoon arrowroot
1 tablespoon cherry brandy
¼ pint double cream

**GM 5 375°F
190°C**

METHOD First make the pastry base. Put the flour in a basin, and rub in the butter until the mixture is like fine breadcrumbs. Scatter in the sugar, and bind the mixture with the egg yolk. Press the dough into a well-buttered 10-inch case. Prick the bottom all over with a fork. Chill while you heat the oven to the given temperature. Bake the case for 30 minutes. Leave in the case for 10 minutes before removing to cool and firm up.

Drain the cherries and stone them. Make a glaze by blending the arrowroot with the cherry juice and heating gently until it thickens. Allow to cool slightly, then add the cherry brandy. Brush a little glaze over the pastry. Place the cherries on top, and spoon the remaining glaze over them. Whip the cream until stiff, and pipe in a border round the edge of the flan.

## PIPED BISCUITS
## SPRITS

*About 25 biscuits*

*These are ideal with steaming coffee or rich hot chocolate flavoured with rum.*

## Ingredients

6 ounces butter
4 ounces castor sugar
A few drops vanilla essence
1 beaten egg
8 ounces plain flour

METHOD Cream the butter, add the sugar gradually, and cream together until light. Add the essence and the beaten egg. Then stir in the sifted flour lightly. Place the mixture in a pastry forcing bag with a large rose nozzle. Lightly butter a baking sheet. Pipe the mixture on to the sheet in short lengths side by side, touching so that they form a long strip 1½ inches wide. The lines of piping go across the width of the strip.

102

Cool the mixture. If possible, chill in a refrigerator. Bake in a moderate oven for 20 minutes, or until pale golden brown. Cut into biscuits while still warm.

## DUTCH DOUGHNUTS
## OLIEBOLLEN

*18 doughnuts*

METHOD Mix the yeast with a teaspoon of the sugar, then add the lukewarm milk. Blend in half the flour and a good pinch of salt. Cover and put the mixture in a warm place to rise. Beat the egg and the remaining sugar together. When the dough has risen, mix into it the egg-sugar mixture, the melted butter, the rest of the flour, and the spice and currants. Leave to rise again.

Knead until the dough is smooth and elastic. Divide it into

*Ingredients*
*½ ounce fresh yeast*
*1 ounce castor sugar*
*¼ pint lukewarm milk*
*1 pound plain flour*
*Pinch of salt*
*1 egg*
*2 ounces unsalted butter, melted*
*1 teaspoon mixed spice*
*4 ounces currants*
*Deep oil or fat for frying*
*Castor sugar for dredging*

# Netherlands

18 equal-sized pieces. Roll each into a ball. Leave the balls in a warm place for 10 minutes. Heat the oil or fat to frying temperature. Fry a few doughnuts at a time, turning them as necessary, until they are pale golden-brown all over. Drain on soft kitchen paper. Finally, roll them in castor sugar.

## SPICED COOKIES
## SPECULAAS

**Ingredients**

6 ounces butter
5 ounces soft brown sugar
8 ounces self-raising flour
Pinch of salt
½ teaspoon mixed spice
1 teaspoon ground cinnamon
Grated rind of ½ lemon
4 ounces finely shredded almonds
1 ounce crushed shortbread biscuit crumbs

reduce to
GM 7 425°F  GM 3 325°F
220°C           170°C

METHOD Cream the butter and sugar until light and fluffy. Sift together the flour, salt and spices, and work them into the creamed mixture. Add the grated lemon rind, almonds and crumbs and mix well. Use a little milk to bind the mixture if needed. With a lightly floured rolling pin, roll out the dough to ¾-inch thickness. Preheat the oven.

Cut the dough into fairly large, well-shaped pieces. Reduce the oven heat and bake the biscuits for about 25 minutes or until golden-brown.

## GINGER PIE
## RECOTTER PASTEI

**This is one of several very old Dutch spiced cheesecakes.**

METHOD Make short crust pastry with the flour, salt, butter and water. Roll it out. Line a shallow springform cake tin, 6½ inches in diameter, keeping enough pastry back to form a lid. Mix the curd cheese with the cream, pine kernels, egg whites (beaten until frothy), the sugar and ginger. Add any cider needed to work the whole mixture to a smooth paste (except for the nuts).

Place the filling in the pie crust, and cover with a pastry lid. Glaze with the egg yolk, well beaten. Bake in a moderate oven at the temperature below, for about 45 minutes. Serve warm or cold.

*Ingredients*

**Pastry**
*4 ounces flour*
*Pinch of salt*
*2 ounces butter*
*Water to mix*

**Filling**
*10 ounces curd cheese*
*3-4 tablespoons double cream*
*4 ounces pine kernels*
*2 egg whites and 1 yolk*
*6 ounces Demerara sugar*
*½ ounce ground ginger*
*Cider to mix if required*

**GM 4 350°F**
**180°C**

# Norway

Norway is a spectacular country of sea and mountains, forests, waterfalls and glaciers. Because of a long dark winter from October to April, followed by a summer in which there is practically no darkness, the Norwegians like to be out of doors as much as possible in their short spring and summer. They arrange their meals accordingly with a sturdy but quickly prepared breakfast of eggs, cheeses, perhaps fish, a variety of breads and plenty of milk; a brief lunch of coffee and an open sandwich; and an early (5 p.m.) meal of at least two courses. A light bedtime meal of sandwiches, cake and coffee will be served about 9 p.m.

Norwegian and Danish food is often similar, for both countries were once under the same king, but there are certain notable differences. Norway is a great fish-eating country, enjoying the harvest of its cold waters which produce fish of very firm texture. Cod, salmon and trout are particularly popular. The Norwegian seas have also produced great whale-fishermen, and whale meat is found everywhere, looking and tasting rather like beef. Lamb and mutton are the most popular meats, and some game such as reindeer, elk, grouse and ptarmigan. These are often cooked in sweet or sour cream, which figures greatly in the Norwegian diet.

Fresh vegetables are more widely used than in other Scandinavian countries, and raw vegetable salads are popular. Berry fruits grow well in Norway and appear in puddings and in the famous fruit soup, used either at the beginning or end of a meal. Baking is not such a feature in Norway as it is in Denmark, but crispbread and rusks are good, and a number of biscuits which include plenty of butter, almonds and spices.

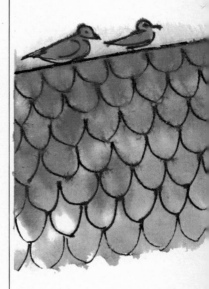

The housewifely art of preserving food in Norway developed because of the long cold winters, the short growing season, and the lack of communications; salting and smoking of fish and meat are good ways of preserving for winter use, and though there is no longer the necessity for this type of preservation, Norwegians still retain a taste for all types of cured and pickled meat and fish.

The pleasure in preserving is also carried over to jam-making, since fruit is very popular. Cranberries, raspberries and strawberries and the stone fruits such as plums and cherries are used for jellies and jams, which often contain rum or brandy. The making of fruit juices and syrups is also popular, and of sharp-flavoured pickles with dill or caraway.

Like all the Scandinavians, the Norwegians like their food to look delicious, and this is clearly shown in their own version of the open sandwich, which looks tempting and has a tasty succulence. One or two of the Norwegian versions are served hot.

A number of recipes in this section are taken from *Norway's Delight* by Elsie Sverdrup, published by Tanum Forlag, Oslo, by kind permission of the author and publisher.

# Norway

## HERRING SALAD

*Ingredients*
2 salt herring
8 ounces cold cooked veal
4 ounces cold cooked potatoes
8 ounces cold cooked beetroot
2 apples
1 large pickled cucumber
4 tablespoons vinegar
4 tablespoons salad oil
1 dessertspoon sugar
4 fluid ounces red wine
Salt and pepper
2 hard-boiled eggs

METHOD Soak the herring in cold water for 12 hours. Dry the fish, bone, and cut into small pieces. Cut veal, potatoes and beetroot into small cubes. Do not peel the apple, but cut into cubes. Cut the cucumber into rings. Mix 2 tablespoons each of oil and vinegar with the sugar and wine, and pour over all the ingredients. Leave to stand in a cold place for 12 hours. Before serving, mix remaining oil and vinegar and cook in a double saucepan over boiling water. Stir continuously until the mixture becomes quite thick. Pour over the salad and garnish with slices of hard-boiled egg.

## SPINACH SOUP
## SPINATSUPPE

*6 helpings*

*Spinach is a favourite vegetable in Norway, and is delicious when made into soup.*

*Ingredients*
2 pounds fresh spinach
3 pints beef or chicken stock
1½ ounces butter
1 ounce plain flour
Salt and pepper
Pinch of nutmeg
2 hard-boiled eggs

METHOD Wash spinach thoroughly and drain well. Chop it coarsely, and drop into boiling stock. Simmer for 10 minutes. Drain, pressing the spinach well, and reserving the liquid. Chop spinach very finely. Melt butter and stir in the flour. Add the hot cooking liquid a little at a time, stirring well. Cover and simmer for 5 minutes, stirring from time to time. Add the spinach, salt, pepper, and nutmeg. Cover and simmer for 5 minutes. Serve garnished with slices of egg.

## FISH SOUP
## FISKESUPPE

*6 helpings*

*There are many popular versions of fish soup. The stock can be made from fish trimmings, which should not be cooked for more than 45 minutes, or the result will be bitter. Parsley stems and celery leaves will give a good flavour to the stock, in addition to onions and carrots.*

*Ingredients*
1 ounce butter
½ ounce plain flour
3 pints fish stock
Salt
2 tablespoons sour cream
1 tablespoon chives, finely chopped
12 small fish balls (see recipe)

METHOD Melt the butter and mix well with the flour. Heat the stock, and add gradually to the flour mixture. Simmer for 5 minutes. Remove from heat and add salt, chives and cream, and fish balls.

## ALE SOUP
## ØLLEBRØD

*4 helpings*

*This beer soup with bread is particularly popular in eastern Norway.*

*Ingredients*
1 pint ale
½ pint water
⅓ pint single cream
2 egg yolks
1 tablespoon sugar
Toasted white bread cubes

METHOD Put ale, water, cream, eggs and sugar into a saucepan, and cook over a very low heat, whipping lightly. Take off the heat when the mixture is about to boil. Serve with toasted cubes of white bread.

## FISH PUDDING OR FISH BALLS
## FISKEPUDDING ELLER FISKEFARSE

*8 helpings*

*A creamy mixture of pounded fish is made into fish pudding or poached fish balls, to be served with melted butter, shrimp, lobster or tomato sauce. When cold, it can be sliced and used as a sandwich topping, or heated in butter.*

# Norway

## Ingredients

2 pounds fresh cod or haddock
2 teaspoons salt
1 ounce cornflour
1 ounce plain flour
Pinch of nutmeg
¼ teaspoon pepper
½ pint milk
¼ pint single cream

**GM 4 350°F
180°C**

METHOD Put the fish through a mincer, and then pound with the salt to a mixture like soft dough. Add cornflour and flour and season with nutmeg and pepper. Gradually work in the milk and cream to make a light, fluffy mixture.

*To make fish pudding*

Grease a 2-pound loaf tin or a mould with butter and sprinkle well with dry breadcrumbs. Put the creamed fish into the container and smooth the top. Cover tightly with cooking foil. Put the container into a baking tin containing boiling water to go about three quarters of the way up the sides. Cook in a moderate oven for 1 hour. The water in the container should simmer, but not boil, or the pudding will have holes. When cooked, the pudding should be firm to the touch, and a skewer inserted will come out clean and dry. Leave pudding at room temperature for 5 minutes, then drain off any liquid, and turn out pudding on to a heated dish.

*To make fish balls*

Chill the fish mixture for about 30 minutes, and then roll a little mixture in the hands to make 1-inch balls. The balls should be kept cold until cooked. Poach in simmering salted water for 3 minutes until firm to the touch. Drain thoroughly.

## NORWEGIAN TROUT
## NORSKØRRET

*4-8 helpings
according to size of fish*

*This recipe may be used for salmon or salmon trout. The fish may be cooked in salted water or in a delicate court bouillon.*

METHOD Put the water, wine, vinegar, quartered onions, diced carrot, celery and herbs into a saucepan and bring to the boil. Cover and simmer for 1 hour, and strain. Meanwhile wipe the fish and wrap in cheesecloth, leaving long ends to use as handles. Put the fish in a deep long kettle or fish boiler on a rack. Put in boiling *court bouillon* and cover pan. Simmer for 8 minutes per pound. Remove fish from pan and unwrap carefully or the skin will come off with the cheesecloth. Curve fish on to a serving dish, and garnish with shrimps, cucumber and mayonnaise, and dill. Other garnishes can include hard-boiled eggs, tomatoes, and smoked salmon.

*Ingredients*
*3 pints water*
*1 pint dry white wine*
*¼ pint white vinegar*
*3 small onions*
*1 carrot*
*½ stick celery*
*1 bay leaf*
*3 sprigs fresh dill (or 1
    dessertspoon dill seeds)*

## HERRING, ANCHOVY AND CAVIARE
## OLSEN'S DREAM

*4 helpings*

METHOD Clean and fillet the herrings. Chop the anchovy fillets finely and spread on the herring fillets together with the caviare. Roll and fasten with cocktail sticks. Coat with the breadcrumbs, and pack tightly into a buttered fireproof dish. Season well with salt and pepper, dot with butter, and pour over the sherry. Bake in a fairly hot oven for 30 minutes.

*Ingredients*
*4 fresh herrings*
*4 anchovy fillets*
*2 tablespoons Norwegian
    caviare*
*2 ounces fine breadcrumbs*
*Salt and pepper*
*½ ounce butter*
*3 fluid ounces sherry*

**GM 5 375°F
190°C**

# Norway

## LAMB AND CABBAGE
**6 helpings** FÅR I KÅL

*Norwegian lamb is excellent and popular. Lamb and mutton are sometimes spiced and cured.*

**Ingredients**

4 pounds breast of lamb
1½ ounces plain flour
2 pounds firm white cabbage
3 sticks celery
Salt
1 pint stock
2 tablespoons whole black peppercorns

GM 4 350°F
180°C

METHOD Trim excess fat from the meat and cut the meat into 2-inch squares. Cook meat in a little hot oil until evenly browned, and then toss meat cubes in flour until evenly coated. In a heavy saucepan, or a large casserole, arrange a layer of meat. Top with a layer of cabbage cut into 1-inch wedges, and then with chopped celery. Sprinkle with salt. Continue in layers twice more and end with a layer of cabbage. Pour in stock. Bruise the peppercorns lightly with a rolling pin and tie in muslin. Add peppercorns to the pan and cover dish tightly. Either cook on gentle heat for 1½ hours, or bake in a moderate oven for 1½ hours. Serve with boiled potatoes.

## VEAL AND PORK BALLS
**8 helpings** MEDISTERKAKER

*Meat balls are popular in all the Scandinavian countries. This Norwegian version is very good served with cooked prunes, apple sauce and cabbage.*

**Ingredients**

8 ounces veal
1 pound lean pork
1 teaspoon salt
½ teaspoon pepper
2 tablespoons dry biscuit crumbs
8 fluid ounces milk
Butter for frying

METHOD Mince the veal and pork together three times. Add seasoning and crumbs, and stir in milk a little at a time. Form into small round balls and cook until brown in butter, shaking the pan so that the balls remain round.

## ROAST VENISON
**8 helpings** DYRESTEG

*Venison and reindeer are popular, particularly with a sour cream sauce.*

**Ingredients**

4 pounds saddle or haunch of venison
4 ounces softened butter
Salt and pepper
½ pint stock
1 tablespoon plain flour
3 fluid ounces thick sour cream
1 ounce goat cheese (Gjetost)

GM 8 450°F
230°C
reducing to
GM 5 375°F
190°C

METHOD Wipe meat well. Spread 3½ ounces butter all over the meat. Roast in a very hot oven for 20 minutes. Reduce heat and sprinkle meat with salt and pepper. Put stock into roasting tin, and roast meat for 2 hours, basting occasionally with pan juices. Put meat on to a heated serving dish.

Melt remaining butter and work in flour, and cook this mixture for 5 minutes on a low heat until it is brown. Gradually add the pan juices from the meat, and when the sauce is smooth, add the cheese cut in small pieces. Stir again until smooth, and add sour cream. Do not boil when cream has been added. Carve the meat in thin slices and serve the sauce separately.

## CREAMED RICE
## RISKREM

*4 helpings*

METHOD Bring the milk to the boil. Wash the rice thoroughly and scatter it on to the milk. Simmer gently for 1 hour, and season with salt. This makes the basic Rice Porridge.

Whip cream with sugar, stir in the rice mixture, and add chopped almonds. Serve with jam or with fruit sauce.

*Ingredients*
*1 pint milk*
*2 ounces rice*
*Pinch of salt*
*8 fluid ounces double cream*
*1 tablespoon sugar*
*1 tablespoon blanched almonds*

## SOUR CREAM WAFFLES
## FLØTEVAFLER

*6 helpings*

*These waffles can be made in a hand or electric waffle iron. They are usually eaten with cranberry or other tart jam.*

METHOD Beat the eggs and sugar for about 10 minutes until thick and creamy. Sift flour with cardamon or ginger. Fold in small portions of flour and cream alternately. Stir in melted butter, and leave the batter to stand for 10 minutes. Heat the waffle iron, pour in batter, and close top. Cook until golden and crisp.

*Ingredients*
*5 eggs*
*4 ounces castor sugar*
*4 ounces plain flour*
*1 teaspoon ground cardamon*
*    or ginger*
*¼ pint sour cream*
*2 ounces melted fresh butter*

## GRIMSTAD RUSKS

*50 rusks*

*Rusks are very popular to eat with soup and with sweet dishes, and for breakfast. They may be circular or rectangular in shape.*

METHOD Sift flour and baking powder. Stir in sugar and rub in butter. Work in cream to form a dough. Roll out and cut into circles or rectangles. Bake in a fairly hot oven for 15 minutes. Split through the centre with a sharp knife, and place cut side up on baking sheets. Dry in a very cool oven until crisp and golden. Store in airtight tin.

*Ingredients*
*12 ounces plain flour*
*2 teaspoons baking powder*
*4 ounces sugar*
*4 ounces butter*
*8 fluid ounces single cream*

GM 5 375°F
        190°C
reduce to
GM 1 275°F
        140°C

# Norway

**PARTY CAKE**
*16 helpings* **KRANSEKAKE**

*This is a celebration cake made from circles of baked almond paste formed into a tower, which can be two feet tall, with a piping of white sugar icing. It is often finished with a decoration of small national flags and sweets. It is most easily made with commercial almond paste. This cake is a favourite at weddings, birthdays and at Christmas.*

*Ingredients*
*3 pounds almond paste*
*8 egg whites*
*1½ pounds icing sugar*

METHOD Put the almond paste in a warm place until very pliable. With a wooden spoon, blend in 4 egg whites. Knead the paste hard with the hands until smooth and firm. Dust a board with icing sugar, and also coat hands with icing sugar. Keep them well coated during the working of the paste. Shape the dough into twelve ½-inch thick rolls of varying lengths: 5, 6, 7, 8, 10, 12, 14, 16, 18, 20, 22 and 24 inches. Put a sheet of brown paper on each baking sheet, and grease and flour it well. Put a roll on each sheet and shape into a ring, pinching the ends together. Pinch each ring with thumb and forefinger with an upward movement, so that rings slope upwards to a sharp crease. Bake in a cool oven for 20 minutes until light golden. Remove from tin and cool on a smooth surface.

Stir icing sugar into remaining egg whites, and beat until smooth. Use two-thirds of the icing to drizzle over each ring in thin trails with a spoon. Put the largest ring on to a serving plate. Thinly spread with a little of the remaining icing. Put next largest ring on top, and repeat process, ending with the smallest ring. The smaller rings may be served whole, and the larger ones divided into sections.

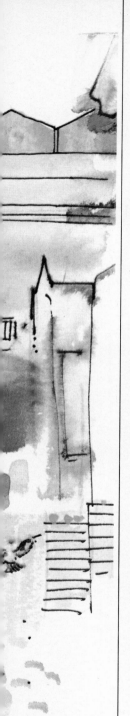

# United Kingdom

True British food derives from a high standard of raw materials cooked in a simple way. The British have always relied on the sparkling fresh sea and river fish; on first class beef, lamb, mutton and pork; plump poultry; rich dairy produce; fine corn; and a wide variety of fruit and vegetables. There is a great emphasis on seasonal foods especially in the country where hunting, shooting and fishing seasons are carefully observed, and the first produce of kitchen garden and orchard eagerly awaited. Throughout the year, festivals of rejoicing, many connected with the Church, are traditionally associated with appropriate food.

Christmas brings its turkey and plum pudding, cake and mince pies; Easter has its Hot Cross Buns and Simnel Cake, formerly eaten on Mothering Sunday in Lent. Whitsun brings Aylesbury duck and gooseberry pie, Michaelmas used to bring a goose with sage-and-onion stuffing and apple sauce. No Hallowe'en (October 31st) would be complete without apples and gingerbread, while a special type of gingerbread called Parkin, and treacle toffee accompany the bonfires of Guy Fawkes Day (November 5th).

The British have always been a meat-eating nation, and perfected the art of roasting. Puddings and pies, potted and pickled meats and fish have developed in the many rural regions, and are common in all types of household. Until the late 19th century large areas of Britain were still mainly agricultural. Rich people were able to benefit more from the exotic spices, tea, coffee, rice and cocoa which stemmed from Britain's international trade.

British food can help in withstanding dark winter mornings and evenings, and the constantly changing weather. Few nations offer such a variety of puddings for the sweet tooth; they are based on native cereal products together with home-produced fats and eggs, but supplemented by vast quantities of imported sugar and chocolate, spices and dried fruit to which the British Isles had easy access.

A hearty breakfast also developed to provide central heating for the rural worker and the sportsman. A variety of good cooked dishes, porridge and toast, and plenty of hot drinks give a warm and encouraging start to the day. At the end of a chilling afternoon in the open air, what can be more welcome than tea-time, with its vast selection of home-baked cakes, biscuits and bread, scones and crumpets oozing with butter and home-made jam?

# United Kingdom

**6 helpings**    **POTTED SHRIMPS**

*This dish must be made with freshly-boiled small pink or brown shrimps, and is traditionally made at Morecambe Bay in Lancashire. The shrimps can be eaten as a first course with thin brown bread and butter, or toast, or they can be used for brown bread sandwiches.*

**Ingredients**
1 pound shelled cooked shrimps
10 ounces butter
½ teaspoon ground mace
½ teaspoon ground nutmeg
Pinch of Cayenne pepper

METHOD Prepare the shrimps. Put 4 ounces butter into a saucepan, and melt it slowly. Skim off foam and remove butter from heat. Spoon the clear butter into a bowl, and discard the milky solids at the bottom of the pan. Melt the remaining butter over moderate heat. Stir in the spices and add the shrimps. Stir them so they are coated in the butter. Pour into six individual dishes or one large one. Pour the clarified butter over them and leave until cold.

# United Kingdom

## DEVILS ON HORSEBACK

*A small savoury used to be served at the end of traditional English dinners, and this was one of the favourite recipes. Angels on Horseback were oysters wrapped in bacon. These 'devils' are now sometimes served with drinks before a meal.*

METHOD Soak the prunes in a little wine overnight, and then stew these in the wine for 10 minutes. Remove the stones. Wrap each prune in half a rasher of bacon and secure with a cocktail stick. Fry or grill until the bacon is crisp and serve on small pieces of hot buttered toast or fried bread.

**Ingredients**
*12 large prunes*
*Red wine*
*6 rashers streaky bacon*
*Buttered toast or fried bread*

# United Kingdom

## OXTAIL SOUP

*It is said that this soup was introduced to London by Huguenot refugees, who lived in an area by a tannery. The buyers of ox hides gave the tails, for which they had no use, to the refugees, who turned them into a rich and nourishing soup. This is best cooked very slowly, and is excellent when reheated.*

### Ingredients
1 oxtail
2 tablespoons seasoned flour
1 tablespoon dripping or butter
2½ pints water
2 carrots
2 medium onions
1 turnip
1 stick celery
Salt and pepper
3 fluid ounces sherry

METHOD Cut the oxtail into pieces and wipe clean. Toss in a little flour seasoned with salt and pepper and fry gently in dripping or butter until golden brown. Put into the saucepan with the water and simmer for 2 hours. Remove meat from the bones and return to the cooking liquid, together with the vegetables cut into small pieces. Simmer for 45 minutes and put through a sieve. Reheat with seasoning, and stir in sherry before serving. Some people like to remove the larger pieces of tail to eat separately, and to leave the smaller pieces in the soup, still on the bone.

6 helpings ## COCK-A-LEEKIE

*This soup from Scotland occasionally includes 4 ounces of stoned prunes.*

### Ingredients
1 boiling chicken
2 pounds veal knuckle
1 carrot
1 turnip
1 onion
4 leeks
2 ounces rice
2 cloves
Salt and pepper

METHOD Put the chicken in a deep pan with the veal knuckle and cover with water, adding a pinch of salt. Bring to the boil, remove scum, then add the carrot, turnip and the onion which has been peeled and stuck with the cloves. Continue simmering till the chicken is tender, and remove the bird. Clean the leeks, removing outer leaves, and cut into short lengths. Strain the broth and add the leeks and the rice. Boil for a further 30 minutes and season to taste. Cut half the chicken into small pieces (using the remainder for another dish) and put into the soup. Just before serving add a teaspoonful of chopped parsley.

6 helpings ## MULLIGATAWNY SOUP

*This soup was brought into the English kitchen by army families returning from service in India. Other meat, such as chicken, may be used, but mutton is the traditional ingredient.*

### Ingredients
2 pounds mutton
3 pints water
2 apples
2 onions
2 carrots
1 turnip
2 tablespoons flour
1 tablespoon curry powder
Parsley and thyme
1 bay leaf
Juice of ½ lemon
Salt

METHOD Cut the fat from the meat and put it in a pan. Heat until the fat begins to run, then add the apples and vegetables cut in slices. Remove the pieces of fat, and continue frying the vegetables for 15 minutes. Sprinkle in the flour and curry powder, cook for 3 minutes, then add the meat cut in small pieces, the herbs and water. Bring to the boil, remove the scum, cover and cook gently for 3 hours. Strain, rub the meat through a sieve, and return to the pan. When boiling, add the lemon juice and season to taste. Serve with a dish of boiled rice.

Scottish cock-a-leekie soup.

# United Kingdom

**MACKEREL WITH GOOSEBERRY SAUCE**

*This is an unusual combination of fish and fruit. A sauce made from gooseberries or rhubarb was considered to be the best accompaniment to grilled or boiled mackerel. The fish should always be very fresh when cooked.*

**Ingredients**
4 mackerel
Salt and pepper
Flour
8 ounces gooseberries
2 ounces sugar
2 tablespoons water
1 ounce butter
Pinch of nutmeg

METHOD Clean and split the mackerel. Season with salt and pepper, and dust with flour. Grill until golden brown. Cook the gooseberries with sugar and water until tender. Put through a sieve and add butter and nutmeg. Reheat and simmer for 5 minutes. Serve hot or cold with the mackerel.

## ROAST LAMB WITH MINT SAUCE

*8-12 helpings
depending on joint*

*Herbs to flavour meat were once chosen from those on which
the animals had grazed, so that they enhanced the original
flavour of the meat. Thyme or marjoram were used to flavour
mountain lamb, but English lamb mostly comes from the
valleys and is accompanied by the mint on which the sheep
grazed when it grew wild by the rivers.*

METHOD The meat on a shoulder of lamb is succulent and sweeter
than on a leg. It can be boned and rolled for easy carving.
Remove any thick pieces of fat from the joint and put them in
the roasting tin to cook with the lamb. Rub the joint with salt
and pepper and squeeze on the juice of a lemon. Put a sprig of
rosemary under the joint. Put the meat into a hot oven for 10
minutes, then reduce heat to a moderate level and continue
cooking for about 1½ hours according to the size of the joint.
Lamb tastes best if it is still slightly pink near the bone. Put
meat on to a hot serving dish. Drain off excessive fat from the
roasting tin, and add a little vegetable water to the pan drippings
to make thin gravy. Serve with roast potatoes and vegetables in
season, together with Mint Sauce.

To make the sauce, put the freshly chopped mint into a bowl
with sugar and hot water. Stir until sugar dissolves, and add
salt and vinegar.

**Ingredients**
*1 shoulder or leg of lamb
Salt and pepper
Juice of 1 lemon
Sprig of rosemary*

**Mint Sauce**
*1 dessertspoon chopped fresh
    mint
1 teaspoon sugar
1 dessertspoon hot water
Pinch of salt
2 tablespoons wine vinegar*

**GM 7 425°F
          220°C**

**reducing to
GM 4 350°F
          180°C**

## ROAST BEEF WITH YORKSHIRE PUDDING AND HORSERADISH SAUCE

*12 helpings*

*Roast beef with Yorkshire Pudding is perhaps the best-known
British dish. In Victorian times a good family joint would
weigh from 12-24 pounds, and was used up during the week
in a variety of ways. There are dozens of family recipes for
the accompanying Yorkshire Pudding, but all cooks agree
that the batter must be cooked in very hot fat from the meat,
and should preferably be cooked in the meat tin with joint on
a rack above so that the juices drip into the pudding. The
pudding always used to be eaten with gravy immediately
before the meat was served. A sharp-flavoured sauce made
with horseradish and the best English mustard should accompany roast beef, served slightly underdone and in wafer-thin
slices.*

METHOD Put the beef into a roasting tin without any fat. Sprinkle
beef with pepper. Roast in a hot oven for 15 minutes. Lower
heat for the rest of cooking time, allowing 15 minutes to the
pound. Baste meat frequently with pan juices. Beef should be
served underdone, and should be transferred to a heated dish
and left to rest for 15 minutes before carving.

To make the Yorkshire Pudding, sieve flour and salt together
into a mixing bowl. Add the eggs and stir into the flour. Add
half the milk slowly, and stir until the mixture is smooth. Add
the remaining milk slowly and beat batter well and then beat in
the cold water. Fifteen minutes before the beef is cooked, pour
2 tablespoons of its fat into a 10-inch square tin. Put tin into the
oven, and when fat is sizzling hot, pour in the pudding batter.
Bake in top of oven for 30 minutes (the meat is removed 15

**Ingredients**
*5 pounds sirloin of beef
Black pepper
Yorkshire Pudding
4 ounces plain flour
½ teaspoon salt
2 eggs
½ pint milk
1 tablespoon cold water*

123

*Roast beef*
*with Yorkshire pudding.*
*The joint is ready to be carve*

minutes earlier to rest before carving). The pudding should be well-risen, puffy, crisp and brown on top and bottom, and should be served straight from the tin in which it is baked, cut in squares.

If fresh horseradish is to be used for the Horseradish Sauce, the root should remain in cold water for 1 hour, then be washed well, and scraped into very thin shreds with a sharp knife. If bottled horseradish is used, it must be drained and squeezed dry in a kitchen towel. To make the sauce, whip the cream to stiff peaks, and fold in the horseradish, sugar, mustard, salt, pepper and vinegar. Serve cold.

**Ingredients**

*Horseradish Sauce*
*2 ounces grated horseradish*
*¼ pint double cream*
*1 teaspoon sugar*
*½ teaspoon dry mustard powder*
*½ teaspoon salt*
*½ teaspoon white pepper*
*2 teaspoons white wine vinegar*

**GM 7 425°F  reducing to**
**220°C  GM 5 375°F**
**190°C**

## ROAST PORK WITH SAGE AND ONION STUFFING AND APPLE SAUCE

*Roast pork with crisp skin or 'crackling' is usually prepared with a stuffing of sage and onion, and is accompanied by apple sauce. If a loin of pork is used, it can be chined for easier carving, or it can be boned and rolled.*

*8-12 helpings depending on joint*

METHOD The skin of pork should be scored by the butcher with a sharp knife. A little oil rubbed into the skin, and a sprinkling of salt and pepper will give crisp crackling. Cook in a fairly hot oven, allowing 30 minutes per pound. Pork should be well cooked and not pink when served. Drain off excess fat, and use a little vegetable water with the pan juices to make thin gravy.

The stuffing may be put into the pork if it has been boned, or cooked separately in the same oven. Peel the onions, chop them coarsely and simmer in water to cover until soft. Add breadcrumbs, butter, sage, and plenty of salt and pepper. When stuffing is well mixed, insert into the joint before roasting. To cook separately, put into a greased ovenware dish and dot with butter. Cook for 1 hour with the joint.

To make the Sauce, use apples which become fluffy when cooked. Peel, core and slice them. Put into a saucepan with the sugar, lemon juice, cloves and a little water. Simmer until soft, and then beat apples to a pulp. Remove cloves, and stir in butter. Serve hot.

**Ingredients**

*1 leg or loin of pork*
*Oil*
*Salt and pepper*
*2 large onions*
*2 ounces fresh white breadcrumbs*
*3 ounces butter*
*2 teaspoons chopped fresh sage*
*Salt and pepper*

*Apple Sauce*
*4 large cooking apples*
*1½ ounces sugar*
*Juice of ½ lemon*
*4 cloves*
*1 ounce butter*

**GM 5 375°F**
**190°C**

## HAM WITH CUMBERLAND SAUCE

*This sauce is named after the Duke of Cumberland, and it is very good not only with ham or bacon, but also with tongue, game, venison and mutton.*

METHOD Soak the ham for 24 hours. Put into a large pan with cold fresh water to cover it. Bring slowly to the boil, taking off scum as it rises. Reduce the heat, and simmer for approximately 20 minutes per pound. Allow 3 hours for 10 pound ham; 3¼ hours for 11 pound ham; 3½ hours for 12-13 pound hams; 3¾ hours for 14-15 pound hams; 4½ hours for 20-pound ham. A bunch of mixed herbs, or a bay leaf, a little brown sugar, and a few peppercorns may be added to the water. Cool the ham in the cooking liquid.

To make the sauce, shred thinly peeled orange and lemon rinds. Put in a pan, cover with water, and bring to the boil.

**Ingredients**

*Cumberland Sauce*
*2 large oranges*
*1 lemon*
*4 tablespoons water*
*4 tablespoons port*
*2 tablespoons vinegar*
*1 tablespoon sugar*
*1 teaspoon made mustard*
*6 glace cherries*
*Salt and pepper*

Simmer for 5 minutes and drain. Put the rind in a clean pan with port, vinegar, sugar, mustard, chopped cherries, salt and pepper, and simmer for 30 minutes. Put into jars and keep in a cool dry place.

## BOILED BACON WITH PARSLEY SAUCE

*8 helpings*

*A boiled joint of bacon with parsley sauce is usually accompanied by broad beans, added to the bacon liquor 15 minutes before serving time. The bacon can be a boned rolled forehock or a piece of collar, and is best soaked for 4 hours before cooking to remove excess salt.*

### Ingredients
4 pound bacon joint
1 bay leaf
6 peppercorns
1 tablespoon brown sugar

Parsley Sauce
2 ounces butter
2 ounces plain flour
½ pint milk
½ pint bacon stock
Salt and pepper
1 tablespoon chopped parsley

METHOD Soak the bacon joint for 4 hours. Put into a saucepan with fresh cold water, bay leaf, peppercorns and sugar. Bring to the boil, then reduce heat and simmer for 2 hours. Drain bacon and strip off skin. Sprinkle fat surface of bacon with a little oatmeal or browned breadcrumbs.

To make the sauce, melt the butter and stir in the flour gradually, away from the heat, until the mixture is smooth. Add milk and stock gradually, beating well, and stir over low heat until boiling. Simmer gently, stirring often, and add parsley, salt and pepper to taste.

## PIGEON PIE

*6 helpings*

*This is good eaten hot or cold. The classic decoration used to be some of the birds' feet stuck through the piecrust in a ring round the pie-funnel.*

### Ingredients
3 pigeons
8 ounces rump steak
4 ounces ham or lean bacon
4 ounces mushrooms
2 hard-boiled eggs
Salt and pepper
¾ pint beef stock
8 ounces puff pastry
1 egg yolk

**GM 7 425°F
220°C
reducing to
GM 4 350°F
180°C**

METHOD Cut each pigeon into four pieces. Cut steak into squares, and ham or bacon into strips. Chop the mushrooms roughly, and cut eggs into quarters. Put steak into the bottom of a pie dish, and then add the pigeon pieces, ham or bacon, mushrooms and eggs. Season well with salt and pepper and pour in the stock. Roll out pastry and cover pie, using pastry trimmings to make decorative 'leaves' to finish the crust. Brush pastry with the egg yolk beaten with a pinch of salt. Bake in a hot oven for 15 minutes, then lower heat to a moderate level for 1¼ hours.

## RAISED PORK PIE

*6 helpings*

*Pork pies appear in different forms in almost every English county, but they are particularly good in the Midlands. The rich pork filling surrounded by savoury meat jelly is enclosed in a very rich pastry made by the hot water method and raised by hand, and the pie is eaten cold.*

METHOD Bring lard and water to the boil in a pan, stirring all the time. Add salt and flour to make a smooth, stiff paste, working with the hands until there are no cracks in the dough. Cover with a cloth and leave for 30 minutes in a warm place. Dice the meat, keeping the fat and the lean separate. Cook the pigs' feet in 1 pint water for 1½ hours to make a stock which will jelly when cold. When the paste is just warm, mould it into a pie casing with a round bottom and straight sides over a traditional wooden mould, or over a jam jar or cake tin, retaining enough to make a lid. Put the meat inside, in layers of lean and fat alternately, season well and moisten with a little stock. Cover with the remaining pastry, sealing the edges, and making a small hole in the top. Tie a piece of greaseproof paper round the pie to keep it in good shape. Bake in a moderate oven for 2 to 2½ hours, and leave until cool. Pour more stock through the hole at the top and leave until cold.

*Ingredients*
*5 ounces lard*
*½ pint water*
*1 pound plain flour*
*½ teaspoon salt*
*1 pound pork*
*Salt and pepper*
*2 pigs' feet*
*1 pint water*

**GM 4 350°F**
**180°C**

## CORNISH PASTIES

*4 helpings*

*These originated as a convenient way of carrying a complete meal for outdoor workers. Each member of the family used to have his initial marked at one end of the pastry.*

### Ingredients
*1 pound plain flour*
*1 teaspoon salt*
*6 ounces lard*
*4 tablespoons finely grated suet*
*Water to mix*
*2 large potatoes*
*1 small turnip*
*1 onion*
*12 ounces lean chopped steak*
*Salt and pepper*

**GM 8 450°F**
**230°C**
**reducing to**
**GM 4 350°F**
**180°C**

METHOD Mix the flour and salt, rub in the lard and add the suet. Mix to a stiff paste with water, and roll out to $\frac{1}{4}$-inch thickness. Cut into rounds, using a plate to cut the size. Slice the potatoes, turnip and onion finely, and place a mixture down the centre of each round, seasoning well. On top put the chopped meat. Damp the edge of each round, and close each pastry across the top, sealing the edges firmly. Pinch the edges between finger and thumb to give a fluted top. Put on a baking sheet and bake in a very hot oven for 10 minutes. Reduce the heat to a moderate level and continue cooking until the meat is tender (about 45 minutes).

*6 helpings*

## LANCASHIRE HOT-POT

### Ingredients
*10 large potatoes*
*6 onions*
*3 lambs' kidneys*
*2 pounds neck of mutton chops*
*Salt and pepper*
*Water*

**GM 7 425°F**
**220°C**
**reducing to**
**GM 2 300°F**
**150°C**

METHOD Peel and slice potatoes and onions, skin and slice the kidneys. Place the chops in the bottom of a casserole, cover with alternate layers of potatoes, onions and kidneys, seasoning well. Cover with a layer of potatoes, and brush well with melted butter. Add a little water, and cook with lid on in a hot oven for 30 minutes, then in a cool oven for 2 hours. Remove the lid for 30 minutes before serving to brown the top. Serve with pickled red cabbage.

*8 helpings*

## BOILED BEEF AND CARROTS WITH DUMPLINGS

### Ingredients
*4 pounds salt beef brisket or silverside*
*1 bay leaf*
*Parsley and thyme*
*10 peppercorns*
*4 onions*
*12 carrots*

**Dumplings**
*4 ounces self-raising flour*
*Water to mix*
*2 ounces suet*

METHOD Tie the meat into a neat shape and put in a large pan with enough water to cover. Add the bay leaf, thyme, parsley and peppercorns, and bring to the boil. Skim, then simmer for $1\frac{1}{2}$ hours. Add the whole onions, and the carrots cut in pieces, and cook for 15 minutes. Make the dumplings by mixing the flour, finely chopped suet and water into a firm paste, and rolling with the hands into eight round balls. Drop the dumplings into the liquid with the meat and vegetables and continue cooking for 30 minutes. Remove the meat to a serving dish, surround with the vegetables and dumplings, and serve some of the cooking liquid.

*8 helpings*

## STEAK AND KIDNEY PUDDING

***This dish was particularly popular in Victorian England.***

### Ingredients
*8 ounces suet*
*1 pound self-raising flour*
*Water to mix*
*2 pounds rump steak*
*2 veal kidneys*
*Oysters or mushrooms if liked*
*Salt and pepper*
*1 bay leaf*

METHOD Chop the suet finely and rub into the flour, than add enough water to make a stiff paste which can be rolled out on a floured board. Roll out $\frac{1}{4}$-inch thick, giving enough paste to line and cover a 2-pint pudding basin. Line the basin with the paste, and fill with alternate layers of steak and kidney cut in small pieces. If oysters are added, they should be put in raw; mushrooms should be sliced and tossed for 2 minutes in a little butter. Season the layers with salt and pepper, and insert the bay leaf

Lancashire hot-pot.

# United Kingdom

half way up. When the basin is full, put in enough water to reach within an inch of the top, moisten the edges of the lining paste and put on the top, cutting off the surplus and pinching the two edges together. Wring out a cloth in hot water, flour it, and tie over the top of the basin with string. Bring up the ends of the cloth and knot on top of the pudding, and then put the basin in a pan of boiling water and boil for 4 hours. The water in the pan must be topped up with boiling water from time to time. When ready for serving, untie the cloth and make a small cut in the top paste to let the steam escape. Serve in the pudding-basin with a table-napkin wrapped round it.

*Roast pheasant with game chips and bread sauce.*

## ROAST TURKEY WITH CHESTNUT STUFFING, SAUSAGE STUFFING AND CRANBERRY SAUCE

*12 helpings*

*This is the traditional British Christmas dish, the bird filled with two stuffings, and accompanied by Cranberry Sauce, Bread Sauce (see Roast Pheasant recipe), a garland of sausages, gravy made from the giblets, roast potatoes, and Brussels sprouts cooked with chestnuts. A turkey can weigh anything from 6 to 36 pounds, but usually has a better flavour when smaller.*

METHOD Wipe the drawn and trussed bird inside with a cloth wrung out in hot water. Put the giblets in a pan with water to make stock for stuffings and gravy. Put *Chestnut Stuffing* into the crop of the bird, pressing it into a smooth rounded shape. Put *Sausage Stuffing* at the other end of the bird. Spread the skin of the bird thickly with butter and sprinkle with salt and pepper. Wrap loosely in foil and cook in a fairly hot oven for 30 minutes. Reduce heat to a moderate level and continue cooking, allowing 15 minutes per pound, and 15 minutes over. Baste frequently, and remove foil 15 minutes before cooking time has finished so that the skin is golden. If sausages are to be served, put them round the bird 30 minutes before cooking time has finished. Serve with gravy made from giblet stock and pan drippings, and with *Cranberry Sauce*, roast potatoes and vegetables.

To make *Chestnut Stuffing*, wash the chestnuts and slit the skins. Cover with water and boil for 15 minutes. Keeping the nuts hot, take out a few at a time and remove outer and inner skins. Simmer the skinned nuts in milk and stock for 15 minutes. Strain and keep the liquid. Crush the nuts. Cut the bacon into small pieces and fry in its own fat until crisp. Add bacon and fat to the nuts, together with breadcrumbs, herbs, lemon rind and seasoning. Bind stiffly with reserved liquid.

To make *Sausage Stuffing*, mix sausage meat with herbs, finely chopped onion, sherry, salt and pepper.

To make *Cranberry Sauce*, put the cranberries in a pan with a little water. Put in a piece of lemon peel and sugar, and simmer for 20 minutes until the skins burst. Take off the heat, and add butter and juice of the lemon. A smooth sauce can be made by rubbing the fruit through a sieve before adding butter and lemon juice.

**Ingredients**
1 10-pound turkey
Salt and pepper
Butter

**Chestnut Stuffing**
1 pound chestnuts
¼ pint milk
¼ pint stock
4 ounces streaky bacon
4 tablespoons white
   breadcrumbs
½ teaspoon mixed herbs
Grated rind of 1 lemon
Salt and pepper

**Sausage Stuffing**
2 pounds sausage meat
1 dessertspoon mixed herbs
1 medium onion
5 tablespoons sherry
Salt and pepper

**Cranberry Sauce**
8 ounces cranberries
1 lemon
2 tablespoons sugar
½ ounce butter

**GM 6 400°F
200°C
reducing to
GM 4 350°F
180°C**

## ROAST PHEASANT WITH GAME CHIPS AND BREAD SAUCE

*4 helpings*

*Pheasant is dry and tasteless if it is eaten without hanging. The birds are hung tail downwards for about seven days, until the leading tail feathers pull out easily. Only young birds should be roasted.*

METHOD Spread a plump young pheasant with butter and put some butter inside the bird. Cover with bacon rashers and roast in a moderate oven for 45 minutes. Remove to warm dish and keep hot. Use the pan drippings with a little stock or vegetable water to make clear gravy, and serve the bird with Brussels sprouts or braised celery.

**Ingredients**
1 pheasant
4 rashers of bacon
2 ounces butter
4 medium potatoes

**Bread Sauce**
*1 medium onion*
*4 cloves*
*½ pint milk*
*Pinch of mace*
*6 peppercorns*
*4 ounces fresh white*
*breadcrumbs*
*½ ounce butter*
*2 tablespoons cream*

**GM 4 350°F**
**180°C**

To make the *Game Chips*, cut peeled potatoes in water-thin slices across. Soak in ice-cold water and dry very thoroughly. Fry in a wire basket in fat heated to 395°F (200°C). Shake the pan as they cook so that they do not stick together. They will float to the surface when ready. Drain on absorbent paper, sprinkle with salt and serve hot.

To make the *Bread Sauce*, stick the onion with cloves and put into a saucepan with the milk, mace and peppercorns. Bring to the boil, and then remove from heat and leave to stand for 30 minutes. Strain the milk into another pan and add the breadcrumbs. Heat until boiling, stirring gently. Stir in butter and cream, and season to taste with salt and pepper.

*6 helpings*

## APPLE CHARLOTTE

*A Charlotte was a type of pudding brought to perfection by the great Carême, at one time French chef at the court of George IV. Either fruit or a type of creamy custard was enclosed in a mould of sponge biscuits. This traditional British version encloses humble apples in a mould of golden butter-crisped bread. The mother and daughter of George IV were both christened Charlotte, so it is possible this type of pudding was named after them.*

**Ingredients**
*2 pounds cooking apples*
*2 ounces butter*
*Thin slices of white bread*
*4 ounces brown sugar*
*Rind of 1 lemon (grated)*
**GM 5 375°F**
**190°C**

METHOD Peel, core and slice apples thinly. Melt the butter, and dip in slices of bread. Line a pie dish or soufflé dish with the buttered bread. Put in apple slices sprinkled with sugar and lemon rind. Cover with buttered bread. Bake in a fairly hot oven for 45 minutes. The bread on the outside should be brown and crisp. Turn out on heated dish and serve with cream or custard.

*4 helpings*

## PANCAKES WITH LEMON AND SUGAR

*These often appear on English tables, but they are specially associated with Shrove Tuesday, or Pancake Day, the Tuesday immediately before the beginning of Lent. The pancakes should be thin and light, and traditionally tossed in the frying pan, though turning with a knife is far easier. They are served sprinkled with sugar and liberally covered with lemon juice.*

**Ingredients**
*4 ounces plain flour*
*Pinch of salt*
*½ pint milk*
*2 eggs*
*Sugar*
*Lemon wedges*

METHOD Sift flour and salt, and lightly beat in milk and egg. Beat with a fork till the mixture bubbles. Heat a frying pan well greased with lard and pour in a little batter. Turn frying pan till the mixture has spread all over the bottom surface. Cook till lightly brown underneath, then turn and cook the other side. Lift out on to a plate and fold. Keep warm while the rest of the batter is cooked, then serve at once with lemon and sugar.

*6 helpings*

## SPOTTED DICK

*Suet puddings cooked in a pudding cloth and shaped like a bolster or long pillow have always been popular in England. They can be made with jam or syrup, or with dried fruit, and*

*Pancakes with lemon and sugar.*

*served with jam or fruit sauce, custard, or with butter and sugar. This version is known as Spotted Dog or Plum Bolster.*

**Ingredients**
8 ounces self-raising flour
4 ounces suet
Pinch of salt
3 ounces sugar
4 ounces currants or raisins

METHOD Mix flour, shredded suet and salt, and work into a dough with cold water to give a soft elastic pastry. Roll into an oblong and sprinkle with sugar and currants or raisins. Roll up and put into a floured cloth. Put on a rack in a saucepan of boiling water and boil for 2 hours. The pudding can also be steamed over a pan of boiling water for 3 hours. Serve in slices with sauce or custard.

8 helpings

## SUMMER PUDDING

*This pudding is best made from a mixture of fresh fruit, particularly raspberries, redcurrants and blackcurrants. Later in the year, it can be made from blackberries, apples, damsons and blueberries. If the fruits are fully ripe and soft, they can be used raw; otherwise they should be cooked gently over a low heat for about 5 minutes.*

**Ingredients**
3 pounds mixed ripe fresh fruit
10 ounces castor sugar
12 ½ inch slices day-old white bread

METHOD Pick over the fruit, discarding any which is unripe or bruised. Put into a bowl with sugar, and leave to stand until the sugar has dissolved. Stir the mixture occasionally. Remove crusts from the bread. Cut one slice into a circle to fit the bottom of a 3-pint pudding basin. Overlap about seven slices of bread round the sides of the basin, trimming them so that they do not overlap more than $\frac{1}{4}$ inch. Put the fruit and sugar into the basin and cover the top with remaining bread. Put a flat plate on top and a heavy weight. Put into refrigerator for at least 12 hours, until the bread has soaked up the fruit syrup. Turn out on to a dish and serve with whipped cream.

## WELSH BARA BRITH

*This is the national bun loaf of Wales. There are sixty varieties of bread and buns in the Welsh-English dictionary, all starting with 'Bara', meaning sustenance.*

**Ingredients**
¼ pint milk
1 ounce yeast
2 pounds plain flour
8 ounces butter
8 ounces brown sugar
Pinch of salt
½ teaspoon mixed spice
12 ounces mixed currants, sultanas, raisins
4 ounces chopped mixed candied peel

**GM 6 400°F 200°C**

METHOD Mix yeast with the warmed milk. Put the flour into a bowl and rub in butter. Add sugar, fruit and spice and mix in the warm liquid. Cover and leave to rise in a warm place for 1½ hours until double its size. Knead into a loaf shape and put into two 1-pound loaf tins. Leave to rise for 10 minutes. Bake in a fairly hot oven for 1 hour. Cool, slice thinly and spread with butter.

## SCONES

*These are the traditional Scottish teatime fare, served with butter, and sometimes with jam and cream as well. The recipe may be varied by adding a little grated cheese or a mixture of currants, sultanas and raisins.*

134

*Welsh bara brith.*

METHOD Sieve flour and add cream of tartar and salt. Rub in butter. Stir soda into milk. Make a well in centre of the flour and add the milk to make a spongy dough, just firm enough to handle. Knead lightly on a floured board and roll out $\frac{3}{4}$-inch thick. Cut in rounds, and bake in a very hot oven for 10 minutes. Cool on a wire rack.

**Ingredients**
*1 pound plain flour*
*¼ teaspoon salt*
*2 teaspoons cream of tartar*
*3 ounces butter*
*1 teaspoon bicarbonate of soda*
*Milk to mix*
*(Milk better sour, then halve*
*  cream of tartar)*

**GM 8 450°F**
**230°C**

## DROP SCONES

*These are best eaten immediately after they have been cooked. They should be wrapped in a clean cloth to cool, so that they remain soft, and should be served slightly warm and spread with butter.*

METHOD Sieve together the flour, salt, soda and cream of tartar. Stir in the sugar and mix to a thick batter with egg and milk. Grease lightly a hot griddle or heavy frying pan with lard, and drop the mixture on with a spoon. When bubbles appear on the surface, turn each scone quickly and cook other side. The scones should be golden brown.

**Ingredients**
*1 pound plain flour*
*½ teaspoon salt*
*2 teaspoons bicarbonate of*
*  soda*
*2 teaspoons cream of tartar*
*1 tablespoon sugar*
*1 egg*
*¾ pint milk*

# United Kingdom

## BATH BUNS

*These buns originated in Bath when it was an eighteenth-century spa. The buns are characterised by a slightly bumpy appearance and a topping of crushed sugar. They contain plenty of dried fruit and candied peel, and sometimes used to include caraway seeds and saffron.*

**Ingredients**
12 ounces plain flour
4 ounces butter
¾ ounce fresh yeast
⅛ pint milk
2 eggs
½ teaspoon salt
3 ounces sugar
Grated rind of 1 lemon
1 ounce chopped mixed candied peel
2 ounces sultanas
Sugar crystals or crushed loaf sugar

GM 8 450°F
230°C

METHOD Rub the butter into the warm flour. Cream the yeast with a little milk and add with the rest of the milk and the eggs to the flour, stirring in the salt. Knead well and leave to rise until double its size. Knead in sugar, lemon rind, peel and sultanas, and make into 10 rough balls. Leave to prove again for 10 minutes. Brush with egg, sprinkle with sugar crystals or crushed loaf sugar, and bake in a very hot oven for 15 minutes.

## YORKSHIRE PARKIN

*This form of gingerbread has always been eaten in Yorkshire and Lancashire on November 5th at firework parties which all England holds to celebrate the unsuccessful attempt by Guy Fawkes to blow up Parliament in 1605 as part of a Roman Catholic conspiracy. Recipes are many and various, and jealously guarded by northern families, the only common agreement being that the parkin should be soft and sticky. This recipe gives a rich dark gingerbread which is hard when baked, but should be kept for a week before eating so that it mellows.*

**Ingredients**
10 ounces fine oatmeal
6 ounces plain flour
1 teaspoon ground cinnamon
2 teaspoons ground ginger
1 teaspoon bicarbonate of soda
1 teaspoon salt
4 ounces soft brown sugar
5 ounces butter
6 ounces black treacle
¼ pint milk
1 egg

GM 4 350°F
180°C

METHOD Mix together dry ingredients except sugar. Warm sugar, butter, treacle and milk until butter has melted. Add to dry ingredients and mix thoroughly. Cool, and add egg. Pour into a buttered 7-inch square tin and bake in a moderate oven for 1 hour.

## DUNDEE CAKE

METHOD Cream the butter and sugar until light and fluffy, and add the eggs one at a time with a sprinkling of flour to prevent the mixture curdling. Beat well after each addition. Stir in most of the flour, the nutmeg, the ground almonds, and lastly the fruit dusted with the rest of the flour. Mix well. Turn into a buttered and lined 10-inch cake tin. Smooth top and arrange the blanched split almonds on it. Bake in a warm oven for 2½ hours.

*Ingredients*
8 ounces butter
8 ounces castor sugar
5 eggs
8 ounces self-raising flour
½ teaspoon grated nutmeg
3 ounces ground almonds
12 ounces mixed currants and
  sultanas
3 ounces chopped glacé
  cherries
2 ounces chopped mixed
  candied peel
2 ounces split blanched
  almonds

**GM 3 325°F
170°C**

## LEMON CURD

*1½ pounds lemon curd*

*This is delicious on bread or toast, but can also be used as a filling for tarts, or as a sauce for puddings.*

METHOD Put the sugar and butter into a double saucepan over hot water. Grate the lemon rind, and squeeze out the juice. Add rind and juice to the sugar, together with lightly beaten eggs. Cook gently, stirring often, until the mixture is smooth, thick and creamy. Put into small pots and cover. Keep in a cool place, and use within four weeks.

*Ingredients*
1 pound castor sugar
8 ounces butter
4 lemons
4 eggs

## STRAWBERRY JAM

*5 pounds strawberry jam*

METHOD Hull and wash the strawberries. Put into a pan with the lemon juice and simmer gently for 30 minutes until soft. Add the sugar and stir until dissolved. Boil rapidly for 15 minutes. Leave to cool for 15 minutes, stir and put into warm jars.

*Ingredients*
3½ pounds ripe strawberries
3 tablespoons lemon juice
3 pounds sugar

## OXFORD MARMALADE

*6 pounds marmalade*

*Marmalade was introduced to Scotland in the sixteenth century, but was originally made from quinces. Commercially produced orange marmalade appeared at the end of the eighteenth century. A very dark marmalade, with the peel cut in thick chunks, is traditionally associated with Oxford.*

METHOD Wash and wipe the fruit. Cut in half and squeeze out the juice and pips. Cut the peel into thick shreds and put into a pan with the pulp, juice and water. Tie the pips into a piece of muslin and put into the pan. Boil gently for 2 hours, until the mixture is reduced by half. Take out the bag of pips and squeeze it well so that the liquid goes back into the pan. Add the sugar and stir until dissolved. Simmer for 1½ hours until the marmalade is dark and has reached setting point. Leave to stand for 15 minutes, stir, and put into warm jars. Cover with lids.

*Ingredients*
2 pounds Seville oranges
1 lemon
4 pints water
4 pounds sugar

# West Germany

Although there are characteristics that are common to the whole of German cooking there are wide regional variations. It is only in comparatively recent history that the many tribes have been united to form the German nation and in each locality the tendency is still to use the local produce cooked in the traditional ways. Nevertheless since Roman times the gradual increase in trade has introduced new ingredients and new cooking methods which have been gradually adopted and adapted to blend in with the native cuisine.

Germans have hearty appetites which they satisfy with generous helpings, often quite simple but very nourishing and frequently including unusual but interesting blends of flavours. They place great emphasis on the careful preparation of fresh ingredients.

In all except the larger towns where distances prevent all working members of one family from returning home for the midday meal, lunch is still the principal meal of the day. It starts with a thick vegetable soup, perhaps with an egg or dumplings in it. The main course is usually a meat dish with vegetables and nearly always includes potatoes or dumplings. This may be followed by a pudding or fresh fruit. Afternoon tea or 'Kaffee' is the occasion for eating the delicious patisserie for which Germany is famous. In contrast the evening meal is often simple, consisting of cold meats, bread and a glass of beer.

The word 'delicatessen' has been given to the world by the Germans which is understandable as their range of cold meats is without equal. There are countless varieties of German sausage or 'wurst'; but they fall into the following three main categories: *Rohwurst* are preserved by smoking and air drying and keep for a long time when stored in a cool place. *Brühwurst*, which are smoked briefly and then parboiled; and *Kochwurst*, which are prepared by boiling. Both *Brühwurst* and *Kochwurst* must be eaten fresh.

There is a gradual change of diet as one moves from north to south. Pork is universal but in the north the climate and soil favour the cultivation of green vegetables and the rearing of healthy cattle for beef and veal. Fish is plentiful from both the North and Baltic Seas, and shellfish abound along the coastline. In contrast further south the food is much richer and vegetables are not often used. The range of sausages increases, river fish replace the sea fish, and on the lush green pastures of the Bavarian hills dairy cattle yield the rich cream which is used in so many of the recipes.

The German has a wide choice of drinks to accompany his food. The national drink is of course beer, of which there are many varieties often named after the towns of their origin. Germany also has its native vineyards based principally on the banks of two of its major rivers, the Rhine and the Moselle. The wide variety of soil, climate, type of grape and the method of harvesting results in thousands of different wines many of which are internationally famous. Finally, we must not forget the local spirits or *Schnapps*.

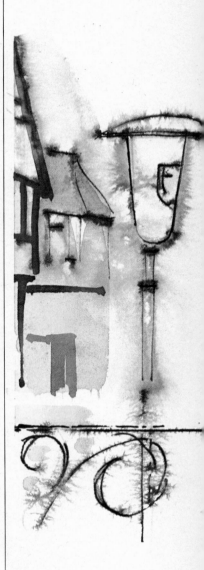

# West Germany

## PICKLED EGGS WITH MUSTARD
## SOLEIER MIT MOSTRICH (SENF)

*6 helpings*

*You see pickled eggs for sale in every Berlin bar. It is most important that the liquid covers the eggs the whole time.*

**Ingredients**

2 pints water
4 tablespoons salt
1 tablespoon caraway seeds
1 onion thinly sliced into rings
10-15 fresh eggs

METHOD Boil the water, salt, caraway and onion for 5-10 minutes. Allow to cool and then strain. Hard boil the eggs for 10 minutes, cool under cold running water and then prick several holes in the shells at both top and bottom. Put the eggs in a jar, cover completely with the liquid and allow to stand for three days, after which time they are ready to use. These eggs can be eaten just with mustard or with a piquant sauce of mustard, pepper, vinegar, sugar and oil. Serve black bread and butter with them.

## LIPTAUER CHEESE

*3-4 helpings*

*By using equal quantities (8 ounces each) of butter and cheese it is possible to transform this recipe into a cheese dip.*

**Ingredients**

8 ounces cottage cheese
2 ounces butter
2-3 anchovy fillets
1 tablespoon gherkin
1 tablespoon chives
1 level teaspoon mustard
Salt and paprika
Lettuce leaves

METHOD Sieve the cheese and beat a little at a time into the well-creamed butter. Drain and finely chop the anchovies. Finely chop the gherkins and chives. Stir in the anchovies, gherkins, chives, mustard, salt and paprika. Roll the cheese into small balls about the size of a walnut. Arrange the cheese, lightly dusted with paprika, on crisp lettuce leaves. Serve with buttered rye bread.

## SMOKED TONGUE SALAD

*2 helpings*

*The German housewife knows instinctively how to utilise small quantities of 'left-overs'. Cold cooked beans, carrots, cauliflower, peas or asparagus may be substituted for the potatoes and celery.*

**Ingredients**

½ pound sliced ox tongue
½ pound mixed cold boiled potatoes and cold cooked celery
3 tomatoes, blanched and peeled
Meat stock
Mayonnaise
Salt and pepper
Finely chopped parsley and capers
1 small onion

METHOD Cut the tongue into fine strips and put in a basin with the roughly chopped potatoes and celery. Add the tomato and grated onion. Barely cover with meat stock. Allow to stand for half an hour then pour away any excess liquid. Stir in a little mayonnaise. Season well. Garnish with the finely chopped capers and parsley.

*A German cold buffet.*

# West Germany

## ASPARAGUS SALAD
### LAMPERTHEIMER SPARGEL ALS SALAT

*4 helpings*

*Choose asparagus in spring for then it is at its best. When buying make sure that the stems are not dry. Scrape the thin stems with a sharp knife starting just below the head or, if the stems are large, peel them thinly. Cut off the tough ends but use them to flavour soups.*

**Ingredients**

6 tablespoons oil
3 tablespoons vinegar
1 tablespoon chopped parsley
Salt
Sugar
1 pound asparagus
2 hard-boiled eggs, shelled
Sour cream, optional

METHOD Simmer asparagus in salted water for about 25 minutes, drain well and refresh under cold running water. Whisk together the oil, vinegar, parsley and a little salt and sugar. Lay the asparagus in a serving dish, pour over the dressing. Chop the eggs and sprinkle over the top. A little sour cream may also be added to this salad. Serve with cooked ham, plain or pickled tongue.

## HARICOT BEAN SOUP
## GRÜNE BOHNEN SUPPE

*8 helpings*

### A warming soup for a cold winter evening.

METHOD Brown the bones and meat in the oven (exact temperature of no importance) before using them. Put them into a large saucepan with the rest of the ingredients, bring to the boil and remove any fat from the top with a spoon. Simmer for 4-5 hours with a tightly fitting lid on the pan. Strain and skim off the fat, cut the meat into pieces and add to the stock. Fry the bacon gently in its own fat add to the stock with the beans and apple. Simmer for about 45 minutes. Season well before serving.

### Ingredients
1 pound marrow bone or
   knuckle of veal
1 pound shin of beef
3 pints water
A bouquet garni—
1 carrot, peeled and sliced
1 onion, peeled and chopped
1 stick of celery, scrubbed and
   sliced
½ tablespoon salt
2 ounces streaky bacon
1 pound fresh haricot beans
½ pound dessert apples,
   peeled and sliced

# West Germany

### LIGHT DORTMUND BEER SOUP
### DORTMUNDER BIER SUPPE

*4 helpings*

*German beers are justly famous, so it is natural that they should be used in cooking. There are many variations but here is a typical one.*

**Ingredients**
6-8 lumps of sugar
1 lemon
2 pints German Lager Beer
Large stick of cinnamon
4 cloves
Pinch of salt
4 teaspoons cornflour
4 eggs, separated
1 tablespoon castor sugar
Cinnamon sugar

METHOD Rub the sugar lumps over the surface of the lemon. Bring the beer to the boil with the cinnamon, cloves and sugar lumps. Add a pinch of salt. Blend the cornflour with a little water and thicken the soup with it. When cooked turn down the heat and whisk in the four beaten egg yolks. Do not reboil the soup or the yolks will curdle. Whisk the egg whites with the tablespoon of sugar to a very stiff snow. Drop spoonfuls of this snow into simmering water and allow them to set. The 'snow dumplings' are then placed on top of the soup and sprinkled with a little cinnamon sugar.

### GREEN PEA SOUP WITH SOUR CREAM
### ERBSENSUPPE MIT SAURERSAHNE

*6 helpings*

*Garnish this soup with toasted squares of white bread or in the South German fashion with strips of smoked tongue. When peas are out of season use the frozen variety but season well.*

**Ingredients**
1 pint shelled peas
1 pint stock or water
1 egg yolk
1 ounce butter
1 ounce flour
¼ pint sour cream
1 tablespoon chopped parsley
Salt, pepper and a pinch of sugar

METHOD Cook the peas in boiling stock or water until they are tender. Put aside to cool. Beat the eggs with the butter and the flour and pour into the cooled soup. Pass through a sieve and reheat. Mix the cream and parsley together and add to the soup. Season well. Sometimes a little cooking sausage is added to improve the flavour of this soup.

### PLAICE WITH FRIED BACON
### SCHOLLE MIT SPECK GEBRATEN

*1 helping*

*The North Germans love their fish fresh. Some even travel to the quayside to be sure of getting it at its best.*

**Ingredients**
1 plaice
Salt and freshly ground black pepper
Lemon juice
2 rashers lean streaky bacon, diced
1-1½ ounces butter
Flour
Chopped parsley

METHOD Wash the fish, rub well with salt, pepper and the lemon juice. Allow to absorb this for 20 minutes, then wipe dry. Fry the bacon gently in the butter for a few minutes, remove and keep warm. Coat the fish in the flour and fry in the bacon fat until golden brown on both sides. Drain on absorbent paper and lay the fish on a heated plate. Sprinkle over the chopped parsley and the bacon. Garnish with lemon slices and serve a potato salad separately.

### FRIED TROUT WITH ALMONDS
### FELCHEN MIT MANDELN

*4 helpings*

*A simple way of serving trout which is popular in the region of Lake Constance. A species of trout known in German as* felchen, *commonly found in that area, is often used for this dish.*

144

METHOD Clean the fish but leave the heads on. Wash and wipe them. Rub the insides of the trout (or *felchen* if available) with salt, white pepper and lemon juice. Coat the fish in seasoned flour. Melt 4 ounces butter in a large frying pan and fry the fish in it two at a time, turning them once until they are tender and golden on both sides about 12 minutes. Drain and keep warm on a serving dish. Clean out the pan and melt the remaining butter, add the almonds and heat until lightly browned, add the remaining lemon juice and pour over the fish. Serve at once with wedges of lemon.

**Ingredients**
*4 trout (about 4-5 ounces each)*
*Salt and white pepper*
*Juice of ½ a lemon*
*Seasoned flour*
*6 ounces butter*
*2 ounces blanched and flaked almonds*

## VEAL FRICASSÉE
## KALBSFRIKASSEE

*4 helpings*

**Chicken makes an ideal substitute if veal is not available.**

METHOD Cut the veal into cubes and toss in the flour. Heat the butter in a flameproof casserole and, when on the point of turning brown, add the meat and fry briskly until golden. Stir in excess flour, pour over the stock and add the herbs, salt and pepper. Cover with a lid and simmer in a warm oven for about 1 hour.

    Put the steak and pork through a mincer, mix with the onion and bind with one egg yolk. Beat well together, add the egg white, shape into small dumplings and poach in boiling water. Take the veal from the pan and thicken the sauce by adding a little cornflour blended with cold water, a beaten egg yolk, lemon juice, salt and pepper. Drain the dumplings and put into the thickened sauce. Return the veal to the pan, reheat and serve.

**Ingredients**
*1 pound veal*
*1 ounce flour*
*2 ounces butter*
*1 pint stock*
*Salt and freshly ground pepper*
*4 ounces stewing steak*
*4 ounces boiling pork*
*1 onion, finely chopped*
*2 egg yolks*
*1 egg white*
*Lemon juice*
**GM 3 325°F**
**170°C**

# West Germany

## BRATWURST WITH RAISINS AND APPLES
## BRATWURST MIT ROSINENÄPFELN

*4 helpings*

*In Germany today there are over 1,000 different varieties of sausage. Bratwurst are made of pork or veal, pink in colour, but the seasoning varies from area to area.*

### Ingredients
1½ pound Bratwurst sausage
1½ pound cooking apples
2 ounces butter
2 ounces sugar
4 ounces stoned raisins

METHOD Grill or fry the sausages until they are golden brown. Peel the apples, core and cut into thick slices. Melt the butter and cook the apples gently in it. Cover with a lid and cook until the apples soften but still have a little shape. Add sugar and raisins and cook a few minutes more. Lay the sausage whole or in thick slices on the bed of apple. Cover and simmer for 10 minutes. Serve with potato dumplings.

## STUFFED BELLY OF PORK
## GEFÜLLTE SCHWEINEBAUCH

*The complementary flavours of pork and apple are well tried but this dish includes prunes in characteristic fashion.*

### Ingredients
4 pounds boned belly of pork,
ready for stuffing
6-8 ounces prunes, soaked
and stoned
½ pound apples, peeled
Cinnamon
Sugar
7 ounces of breadcrumbs
4 eggs
Butter
2 onions, chopped
¾ pint meat stock

GM 3 325°F
170°C

METHOD Lay the meat out flat and cover with the prunes, sliced apples, cinnamon and a little sugar. Blend together the breadcrumbs and eggs and spread over the fruit. Then sew up the meat, rub with salt and brown in a little butter with the onions. After 10 minutes pour over the hot meat stock, add the *bouquet garni,* cover with a lid and continue cooking in a warm oven until tender, about 3 hours. Serve with boiled potatoes and red cabbage.

## ROAST VEAL WITH CREAM SAUCE
## KALBSBRATEN MIT SAHNESOSSE

*8-10 helpings*

*Allow ½ pound of meat with bone per person. To improve the flavour, cover the joint with streaky bacon rashers.*

### Ingredients
A leg of veal
Salt, pepper and paprika
2 ounces butter
1 onion, coarsely chopped
Cornflour
¼ pint sour cream

GM 7 425°F
220°C

METHOD Weigh the joint and calculate the cooking time. Allow 25 minutes per pound plus 25 minutes if the meat is on the bone, 30 minutes per pound plus 30 minutes if the joint is boned and rolled. Season well with the salt, pepper and paprika. Fry the meat briskly in the butter. Place in a roasting tin, add a little water together with the onion and roast in a hot oven for the required time. When the meat is cooked, remove from the tin and keep warm. Blend cornflour with a little water and add to the meat juices with the sour cream. Serve the meat whole or sliced with the sauce poured over. This dish is often served with fried mushrooms.

# West Germany

## KÖNIGSBERG DUMPLINGS
## KÖNIGSBERGER KLOPSE

*A dish from East Prussia that has become world famous.*

METHOD Mince the meat, rolls, onions and anchovy finely, then beat in the eggs, salt and pepper and form small balls from the mixture. Drop them into boiling stock, bring to the boil once and then leave to stand for 20 minutes. When they float to the surface they are ready. Take the 'Klopse' from the stock and keep warm in a serving dish. Pour the stock through a sieve, bring to the boil, thicken with cornflour blended to a smooth paste with cold water. Blend the egg yolks with the sour cream and add to the sauce which should not be cooked any more. Stir in capers and lemon juice. Cover the 'Klopse' with the sauce and sprinkle with chopped parsley. Serve with boiled potatoes.

### Ingredients
½ pound pork
1 pound beef
3 bread rolls, soaked in milk
 and squeezed dry
2 large onions, quartered and
 browned
3 anchovy fillets
2 eggs
Salt and pepper
½ pint stock, approx.

**Sauce**
Cornflour
2 egg yolks
3 tablespoons sour cream
Capers
Lemon juice
Chopped parsley

# West Germany

**6 helpings**

### CASSEL'S RIB OF PORK
### KASSELER RIPPCHEN

*Legend has it that a Berlin butcher named Cassel discovered this recipe when he spit roasted a rib of pork to seal in the juices and then completed the cooking by boiling it.*

**Ingredients**

3¼ pounds smoked ribs of
pork
½ pint hot water
1 onion
1 tomato
1-2 teaspoons cornflour
4-5 tablespoons sour cream

**GM 5 375°F
190°C**

METHOD Remove the bones from the meat and score the surface of the fat with a sharp knife, cutting both ways in a crisscross pattern. Rinse out a roasting tin with water and place the meat, fat side up, on a greased grid in the tin. Place the tin in the middle of a fairly hot oven. As soon as the dripping begins to brown, add a little of the water to the tin. About a quarter of an hour before the meat is done, add the skinned and quartered onion and the washed and skinned tomato. When the meat is tender, after about 1½ hours, turn off the heat. Leave the meat on the grid but take it out of the tin and keep it hot while making the gravy. Place the tin on top of the cooker. Scrape the residue from the bottom and add enough of the remaining water to dissolve the meat juices. Strain through a sieve. Thicken with cornflour blended with cold water and stir in the cream. Serve with creamed potatoes and Brussels sprouts or sauerkraut.

# West Germany

## HEAVEN AND EARTH
## HIMMEL UND ERDE

*4-5 helpings*

*An old peasant dish from the Lower Rhine.*

METHOD Wash the potatoes, boil them in their skins. Peel the apples, quarter, core and stew until soft with a little sugar and water. Meanwhile, slice the black pudding and fry on both sides in half the butter with the onions, until both are crisp. Peel and sieve the potatoes while still hot. Keep hot. Pass the apple through a sieve, then blend into the potato with the remaining butter. Season well with salt, pepper and nutmeg. Arrange the slices of black pudding round the plate, pile the potato in the centre and sprinkle the onions over it all. Serve with home-baked bread and a glass of geneva.

*Ingredients*
*2 pounds potatoes*
*¾ pound apples*
*Sugar*
*½ pound black pudding*
*1½ ounces butter*
*2 medium onions*
*Salt, pepper and nutmeg*

## PEARS, BEANS AND BACON
## BIRNEN, BOHNEN, SPECK

*6 helpings*

*A favourite in Hamburg.*

METHOD Top and tail the beans. If they are large, cut them into small pieces. Peel, core and quarter the cooking pears. Chop the bacon. Melt the butter in a saucepan and fry the bacon gently without browning. Add the beans and pears. Season with salt and pepper. Just cover the pears and beans with sufficient stock. Bring to the boil, cover with a lid and simmer for about 40 minutes. Sprinkle with parsley and serve with boiled potatoes.

*Ingredients*
*¾ pound streaky bacon*
*1 ounce butter*
*1 pound French beans or*
*1 pound runner beans*
*¾ pound cooking pears*
*Salt and pepper*
*Stock*
*Parsley*

## BERLIN KNUCKLE OF PORK WITH
##   PEASE PUDDING AND SAUERKRAUT
## BERLINER EISBEIN

*6 helpings*

*Although this is a Berlin speciality it is to be found on the menu in many other parts of Germany.*

METHOD Wash the knuckle of pork and simmer until tender with the cloves, peppercorns, onion and bay leaf in plenty of water. Heat the dripping and brown the onion in it. Add the sauerkraut, caraway seeds, juniper berries, bay leaf and seasoning. Then add some of the stock from the knuckle of pork and cook slowly. Soak the peas overnight, then bring to the boil with the garlic, lemon peel and one of the onions and cook until soft. Put the peas through a sieve. Finely chop the bacon and the remaining onion and brown together in the dripping, then add to the pease pudding.

*Ingredients*
**Knuckle of pork**
*1 pickled knuckle of pork*
*Some cloves and peppercorns*
*1 onion, chopped*
*1 bay leaf*

**Sauerkraut**
*2 ounces dripping*
*1 onion, chopped*
*1¾ pounds sauerkraut*
*A few caraway seeds and*
*   juniper berries*
*1 bay leaf*
*Salt and pepper*

**Pease pudding**
*1 pound of split yellow peas*
*1 clove of garlic, crushed*
*A piece of lemon peel*
*4 ounces of bacon*
*2 onions, chopped*
*1 ounce dripping*

# West Germany

## VIERLAND DUCK
## VIERLÄNDER ENTE

*4 helpings*

*The marshland at the mouth of the Elbe is famous for its ducks. In this recipe the apple counteracts the tendency for duck to be greasy.*

### Ingredients

1 duck
1 onion
2 ounces butter
6 ounces ham
2-2¼ pound cooking apples
3 tablespoons breadcrumbs
(approx.)
½ teaspoon dried marjoram
Few spikes rosemary
Nutmeg

Garnish
2-3 eating apples, peeled and
cored
2 ounces ham
½ pint sour cream
1 tablespoon flour

**GM 6 400°F
200°C**

METHOD Chop the onion finely and brown in 1 ounce butter together with the finely diced ham and duck liver. Peel, core and grate the apples into the mixture and bind with the breadcrumbs. Season with salt, pepper and herbs. Stuff the duck with the mixture, sew up and truss. Rub the duck with salt, pepper and nutmeg, lay breast side down in a roasting tin. Pour ¾ pint water into the tin and roast in a fairly hot oven, allowing 20 minutes to the pound. To make the garnish cut the apples into slices and fry in 1 ounce butter with the ham. Stir in the flour, pour over the soured cream, season well and serve separately as a sauce. Red cabbage and creamed potatoes go well with this.

## COOKED SAUERKRAUT
## GEKOCHTER SAUERKOHL ODER SAUERKRAUT

*6 helpings*

*Although sauerkraut is probably the best known of all German vegetables it in fact originated in China and was brought to Germany by the invading Tartars.*

### Ingredients

2 pounds sauerkraut
3 onions
2 apples
3 ounces pork dripping
½ pint stock or water
1 onion stuck with 2 cloves
1 bay leaf
3 juniper berries
Salt and sugar
Lean bacon or pork (optional)
1 large potato, or cornflour
Freshly ground black pepper

METHOD Peel and slice the onions and apples in the dripping without letting them colour, then add the *sauerkraut*. Pour over the water or clear stock. Add the onion stuck with cloves, bay leaf, juniper berries, a pinch of salt and sugar. Cover with a lid and cook over a low heat. If water has been used to cover the cabbage, the flavour will be improved if a piece of lean bacon or pork is cooked with the cabbage. As soon as the cabbage is ready, after about 45 minutes, thicken with grated potato or cornflour mixed with a little cold water. Remove the bacon from the sauerkraut and season with salt and freshly ground black pepper.

## RED CABBAGE
## ROTKOHL

*6 helpings*

*Like sauerkraut, red cabbage is best cooked slowly.*

### Ingredients

2 ounces dripping
1 large red cabbage
4 cooking apples, peeled and
chopped
1 onion, chopped
1 teaspoon sugar
A few cloves
Vinegar or water
1 wineglass red wine
(6 fluid ounces)

METHOD Melt the fat in a thick-bottomed saucepan, then add the cabbage, finely shredded, the apples, onion, sugar, cloves, and just enough vinegar or water to prevent burning. Simmer for two hours, add the wine, and continue slowly cooking until the liquid is reduced to nothing.

# West Germany

## THÜRINGIAN POTATO DUMPLINGS
## THÜRINGER KLÖSSE

*2-3 helpings*

*These dumplings may be served whenever boiled potatoes are appropriate. There are many regional variations.*

METHOD Finely grate the potatoes into a bowl of water, then put them into a cloth and squeeze out as much liquid as possible. Bring the milk, salt and the fat to the boil. Add the semolina, stirring all the time until a solid mass has formed. Cook this for about a minute, then remove from the heat and stir into the grated pressed potatoes. With floured hands shape the mixture into four to six balls. Press into each ball a few croûtons, then drop the dumplings into boiling salted water and simmer until cooked.

### Ingredients
1 pound approx. peeled, raw
    potatoes
¼ pint milk
Salt
1 ounce butter or margarine
2 ounces semolina
Flour
Toasted croutons

## GREEN GRAPES IN WINE JELLY
## GRÜNE TRAUBEN IN WEINGELEE

*4 helpings*

*Easy to make but effective for special occasions.*

METHOD Put the water in a small bowl and sprinkle over the gelatine. Put the wine, lemon or orange rind and sugar in a saucepan. Heat until the sugar has dissolved but do not boil. Remove the rind from the pan, add the soaked gelatine and stir until it has dissolved then leave to cool. Halve the grapes if large and remove the pips. If the grapes are the seedless variety leave them whole. Pour the half-set jelly into glasses and add the grapes. Serve with lightly whipped cream and macaroons.

### Ingredients
1½ tablespoons cold water
1½ level teaspoons powdered
    gelatine
½ bottle Silvaner or Gutedel
    white wine (12 fluid ounces)
A strip of lemon or orange
    rind
1-2 ounces castor sugar
½-¾ pound white grapes

# West Germany

### CHESTNUT CREAM
### KASTANIENCREME

*4-6 helpings*

*Time can be saved by using canned chestnut purée; if it is already sweetened, reduce the amount of sugar in the recipe.*

**Ingredients**

2 egg yolks
1½ ounces castor sugar
½ pint milk
2 tablespoons cold water
2 teaspoons powdered gelatine
5-8 ounces chestnut purée from about 1 pound of chestnuts
¼ pint double cream
Vanilla essence
3-4 tablespoons rum

METHOD Whisk the egg yolks and sugar together until light and creamy. Heat the milk and pour slowly over the creamed mixture, whisking all the time. Cook in a double saucepan until the mixture thickens. Put the water in a small bowl, sprinkle over the gelatine and place in a pan with a little hot water and simmer until the gelatine dissolves. Add a little of the thickened mixture to the gelatine and then stir back into the bulk of the mixture. Cool until on the point of setting. Meanwhile roast the chestnuts, remove the outer shell and the inner brown skin. Cook in water until soft, drain, and then rub through a sieve. Stiffly whisk the cream and stir into the setting creamed mixture with a little vanilla essence, chestnut purée and rum.

## ROUNDHEAD KUGELHOPF

8 helpings

*A very traditional dish from the border lands of France and Germany.*

METHOD Sift the flour into a bowl. Hollow out the centre and add 1½ teaspoons of sugar, the yeast and the milk. Blend the yeast and milk together and gradually stir in a little of the flour to make a thick batter. Leave in a warm place for about 25 minutes or until frothy. Add the raisins, remaining sugar, lemon rind and a good pinch of salt and mix in the rest of the flour. Heat the butter until it just melts and add to the dough together with the beaten egg. Beat with a wooden spoon until the dough leaves the sides of the bowl. Knead on a lightly floured surface for about 5 minutes. Butter a 1½ pint ring mould and sprinkle the almonds in it. Fill with dough and put inside a large oiled polythene bag and leave in a warm place to rise. When the dough reaches the top of the tin, remove the polythene bag and bake in a moderate oven for about 30 minutes. Turn out on to a wire rack and sprinkle liberally with sugar.

### Ingredients

½ pound plain flour
1½ teaspoons sugar
½ ounce fresh baker's yeast
4 tablespoons milk
1½ ounces sugar
1½ ounces raisins
Grated rind of half a lemon
Salt
2½ ounces butter
1 egg
2 ounces chopped almonds

GM 4 350°F
180°C

## STRAWBERRY CAKE ERDBEER TORTE

8-10 helpings

*An example of the delicious German patisserie. Serve it with lashings of whipped cream and freshly ground coffee.*

METHOD Oil two 9½-10 inch sponge tins, line the base with greaseproof paper and dust with flour. Sift together the flour, cornflour and baking powder two or three times. Break the eggs into a large bowl and whisk for 1-2 minutes either using electric beaters or a rotary whisk. Place the bowl over a saucepan of simmering water. Add the sugar and whisk over the heat until the mixture is creamy. Remove from the heat and whisk until the mixture is cool and the beaters leave a trail when lifted above the mixture. Gently fold in the flour a little at a time finally adding the grated lemon rind. Divide the mixture between the two tins and bake in a fairly hot oven for about 25 minutes. Remove from the tins and cool on a wire rack.

Spoon the jam and water into a small saucepan, bring to the boil and bubble to a thick glaze. Brush one surface of the sponge with the glaze and sandwich the layers together. Brush the sides with more jam and press the nuts into the sides using a small palette knife. Lift the cake onto a flat serving plate. Arrange the strawberries on top halving them if large, brush with the remaining glaze and serve.

### Ingredients

5 ounces plain flour
2 ounces cornflour
A good pinch of baking powder
Finely grated rind of 1 lemon
5 large eggs
7 ounces castor sugar
8-10 tablespoons strawberry jam
4 tablespoons water
2 ounces blanched and chopped almonds, toasted
1 pound fresh strawberries

GM 5 375°F
190°C

# West Germany

## SAXON CHEESE CAKE
## SÄCHSISCHER KÄSEKUCHEN (QUARKKUCHEN)

*The cheese cake has its origins in ancient history and each country has developed its own variations.*

### Ingredients
**Dough**
½ pound strong plain flour
½ teaspoon sugar
¼ ounce fresh yeast
¼ pint warm milk
½ teaspoon salt
1 ounce butter

**Filling**
3 eggs, separated
4½ ounces castor sugar
1¾ pound curd cheese
Salt
2 ounces plain flour
2½ ounces butter
3½ ounces raisins
Icing sugar

**GM 4 350°F
180°C**

METHOD To make the dough, blend together 2½ ounces of flour, sugar, yeast and milk to a thick batter. Leave the batter in a warm place until frothy (about 20 minutes). Sift the remaining flour and salt and rub in the fat. Add the flour mixture to the batter and mix well to give a fairly soft dough. Knead for about 10 minutes. Place in a lightly oiled polythene bag and allow to rise until double in size. Turn the dough on to a lightly floured surface and knead. Butter an 8¼ inch loose bottom, deep, spring release tin (approx. 4 pint capacity). Line the tin with the dough.

For the filling, whisk the egg whites stiffly, gradually adding the sugar. Sieve the curd cheese and add a little of the whisked egg white to it. Fold the mixture into the bulk of the egg whites with a pinch of salt, flour (adding a spoonful at a time), egg yolks, melted butter and raisins. Turn into the tin and bake in the bottom of a moderate oven for about ¾ hour. Allow to cool, remove from the tin and dust heavily with icing sugar.

## BLACK FOREST CHERRY CAKE
## SCHWARZWÄLDER KIRSCHTORTE

*The Black Forest is famous for its cherries, some of which are made into the Kirschwasser liqueur.*

### Ingredients
**Cake**
3½ ounces plain flour
½ ounce cornflour
½ ounce cocoa powder
2 ounces butter
4 eggs
3½ ounces icing sugar

**Filling**
2 ounces castor sugar
4 tablespoons water
3 tablespoons Kirsch
8 tablespoons cherry jam
½ pint double cream
2 tablespoons milk

**For the Decoration**
Grated chocolate
Cherries
Flaked almonds

**GM 4 350°F
180°C**

METHOD Grease and flour an 8¼ inch loose bottom, deep, spring release tin fitted with the plain base. Sift together the flour, cornflour, and cocoa powder. Heat the butter until it just melts. Break the eggs into a deep mixing bowl, add the sugar and whisk over a pan of hot water until light and fluffy. Remove from the heat and continue beating until the mixture is cool. Fold in the flour alternately with the cool but still flowing butter. Bake in a moderate oven for about 30 minutes. Cool for a short while before turning out.

When cool, slice into three layers. Dissolve the 2 ounces of sugar in the 4 tablespoons of water. Bring to the boil and bubble for 2-3 minutes. Add the Kirsch and sprinkle over the layers. Spread the base and second layer with cherry jam. Stiffly whisk the cream with the milk and spread a little over jam. Sandwich the layers together and mask the cake with more cream. Use the remainder to pipe whirls around the top outside edge. Press the chocolate into the sides and decorate the top with cherries and flaked almonds.

154

# Index

An alphabetical guide to the dishes featured in the book. Please note that there are many dishes where the particular course served varies either between countries, or depending on personal taste. The editors nevertheless hope that this index will be a practical help for the reader.

# Index

# Index

# Index

# Weights and Measures

*British Standard Weights and Measures are used throughout this book. Quantities are given in pounds, ounces and pints, or, where this is not practical, in British Standard Spoon and Cup Measures.*

*The table below shows approximate weights of handy measures using the British Standard Kitchen Measuring cup and tablespoon.*

| FOOD | Weight of 1 level cup | Number of level tablespoons to 1 ounce |
|---|---|---|
| Breadcrumbs – dry | 3 ounces | 3 |
|           – fresh | 2 ounces | 2 |
| Butter and other fats | $9\frac{1}{2}$ ounces | 2 |
| Cornflour | 5 ounces | 3 |
| Flour – unsifted | 6 ounces | 3 |
| Salt | — | 2 |
| Sugar – castor | $7\frac{1}{2}$ ounces | $2\frac{1}{2}$ |
|      – granulated | $8\frac{1}{2}$ ounces | 2 |
|      – demerara | 7 ounces | $2\frac{1}{2}$ |
|      – icing | 6 ounces | 3 |
| Syrup | 14 ounces | 1 |

## LIQUID MEASURES

| | | | | |
|---|---|---|---|---|
| 3 Teaspoons | = | 1 Tablespoon | | |
| 2 Tablespoons | = | $1\frac{1}{4}$ fluid ounces | | |
| 4 Tablespoons | = | $2\frac{1}{2}$ fluid ounces | = | $\frac{1}{8}$ pint |
| 8 Tablespoons | = | 5 fluid ounces | = | $\frac{1}{4}$ pint |
| 16 Tablespoons | = | 10 fluid ounces | = | $\frac{1}{2}$ pint = 1 B.S. Cup |

## DOMESTIC OVEN TEMPERATURES

| Gas Oven Marks | Present Electric Scale | Suggested Celsius Scale |
|---|---|---|
| | 200°F | 100°C *Below thermostat* |
| $\frac{1}{4}$ | 225°F | 110°C     *setting.* |
| $\frac{1}{2}$ | 250°F | 130°C |
| 1 | 275°F | 140°C |
| 2 | 300°F | 150°C |
| 3 | 325°F | 170°C |
| 4 | 350°F | 180°C |
| 5 | 375°F | 190°C |
| 6 | 400°F | 200°C |
| 7 | 425°F | 220°C |
| 8 | 450°F | 230°C |
| 9 | 475°F | 240°C |

*This table is a guide to oven thermostat settings and should be used if your recipe gives temperatures instead of gas marks. The temperatures are given in Fahrenheit and Celsius.*

# *Acknowledgements*

Many people in different countries have helped to create this book. The Publishers would like to thank them all. Thanks in particular are due to:

Miss Wendy Matthews, The Home Service Advisor, British Gas; M. Paul Vanhecke of the Belgian Embassy, London; Miss Pauline Viola; Danish Agricultural Producers for permission to reproduce photographs; Danish Food Centre, London; Allan Brusendorff of Copenhagen.

Mme. Thérèse Rochon of Chez Solange Restaurant, London for providing the following dishes:

Best end of neck *Princesse, Oeufs en meurette*, Crab Montecarlo.

Mrs T. Montgomery and M. Pannier of À L'Écu de France, London for preparation of all other French dishes.

Mrs D. Beresford of the Irish Export Board.

Dr Pannico of the Italian Institute for Foreign Trade; Sgr Guiseppe de Gasperi; Toninos, London; The Pizza House.

M. J. Alex, First Secretary of the Luxemburg Embassy, London; Mme Pescatore of Luxemburg.

Miss Jennifer Vaughan of the Dutch Dairy Bureau; Mrs Audrey Ellison. Roald Dahl, Mr and Mrs Mathisen of the Norway Food Centre, London; J. Hudson and H. Jacobi; Centrale Marketinggesellschaft der deutschen Agrarwirtschaft mbH, for permission to reproduce photographs in the West German section. Fay Godwin for permission to reproduce Jane Grigson's photograph.

Thanks are also due to the following companies for their assistance:

Heal & Son Limited
Kempinski Limited
Royal Copenhagen Porcelain
Meijer Pers (n.v.) of Amsterdam
Josiah Wedgwood & Sons Limited

Finally, the three photographers, John Dixon, Julia Hedgecoe and Peter Esterhazy for their concentrated efforts.